OPEN
MBSR

MO EDJLALI

Founder and CEO of *MINDFUL LEADER*

OPEN MBSR

Reimagining the Future of Mindfulness

WILEY

Copyright © 2025 by Mohammadjafar Edjlali. All rights reserved.

Published by John Wiley & Sons, Inc., Hoboken, New Jersey.
Published simultaneously in Canada.

No part of this publication may be reproduced, stored in a retrieval system, or transmitted in any form or by any means, electronic, mechanical, photocopying, recording, scanning, or otherwise, except as permitted under Section 107 or 108 of the 1976 United States Copyright Act, without either the prior written permission of the Publisher, or authorization through payment of the appropriate per-copy fee to the Copyright Clearance Center, Inc., 222 Rosewood Drive, Danvers, MA 01923, (978) 750-8400, fax (978) 750-4470, or on the web at www.copyright.com. Requests to the Publisher for permission should be addressed to the Permissions Department, John Wiley & Sons, Inc., 111 River Street, Hoboken, NJ 07030, (201) 748-6011, fax (201) 748-6008, or online at http://www.wiley.com/go/permission.

The manufacturer's authorized representative according to the EU General Product Safety Regulation is Wiley-VCH GmbH, Boschstr. 12, 69469 Weinheim, Germany, e-mail: Product_Safety@wiley.com.

Trademarks: Wiley and the Wiley logo are trademarks or registered trademarks of John Wiley & Sons, Inc. and/or its affiliates in the United States and other countries and may not be used without written permission. All other trademarks are the property of their respective owners. John Wiley & Sons, Inc. is not associated with any product or vendor mentioned in this book.

Limit of Liability/Disclaimer of Warranty: While the publisher and author have used their best efforts in preparing this book, they make no representations or warranties with respect to the accuracy or completeness of the contents of this book and specifically disclaim any implied warranties of merchantability or fitness for a particular purpose. No warranty may be created or extended by sales representatives or written sales materials. The advice and strategies contained herein may not be suitable for your situation. You should consult with a professional where appropriate. Further, readers should be aware that websites listed in this work may have changed or disappeared between when this work was written and when it is read. Neither the publisher nor authors shall be liable for any loss of profit or any other commercial damages, including but not limited to special, incidental, consequential, or other damages.

For general information on our other products and services or for technical support, please contact our Customer Care Department within the United States at (800) 762-2974, outside the United States at (317) 572-3993 or fax (317) 572-4002.

Wiley also publishes its books in a variety of electronic formats. Some content that appears in print may not be available in electronic formats. For more information about Wiley products, visit our web site at www.wiley.com.

Library of Congress Cataloging-in-Publication Data is Available:

ISBN 9781119988632 (Cloth)
ISBN 9781119988649 (ePub)
ISBN 9781119988748 (ePDF)

Cover Design: Jon Boylan
Cover Image: © mailvelous/Shutterstock

SKY10119376_062125

To Samir and Daria, my precious children: You remind me daily how to stay present, embrace wonder, and find joy in life's smallest moments.

Contents

Prologue: The Moment Everything Changed   ix
Introduction   xi

Part I   A Starting Point   1
1. The Basics   3
2. What Is MBSR?   23
3. Buddhist Roots of MBSR   41
4. Inspirations from Unlikely Sources   63

Part II   The Three Fundamental Problems   87
5. Buddhist Entanglement   89
6. Beyond Black and White   109
7. Oligarchy: The Hidden Hand   133

Part III   The Open MBSR Framework   157
8. The Open MBSR Manifesto   159
9. Open MBSR Teaching Essentials   177
10. Charting the Path Forward   201

A Personal Note to Readers	213
Notes	215
References	217
Acknowledgments	221
About the Author	223
Index	225

Prologue: The Moment Everything Changed

The best way to fool someone into sleepwalking is to convince them they're awake. Just like in Christopher Nolan's film *Inception*, the deepest dreams are the ones where we believe we've risen to consciousness. I discovered this truth in a familiar San Francisco conference hall, watching my mentors and colleagues deliver polished talks about presence and authenticity, when suddenly the carefully constructed facade cracked. Behind the curated smiles and secular language, I saw what we'd become: a movement that had recreated the very power structures it had originally sought to dismantle.

The irony wasn't lost on me. For over a decade as the leader of Mindful Leader, I'd helped build this world. Like so many others, I'd been drawn to mindfulness by its revolutionary promise: a scientifically validated path to greater awareness, free from religious dogma and guru worship. It offered a bridge between ancient wisdom and modern neuroscience, a way to foster genuine human connection in an increasingly disconnected world. Yet here we were, unconsciously fostering dependency, elitism, and what some might call spiritual materialism.

This unsettling realization couldn't have come at a more critical moment. We stand at the precipice of humanity's most profound transformation since the invention of agriculture: the AI revolution. Our new systems aren't just handling routine tasks—they're writing poetry, diagnosing diseases, and solving complex problems that once defined human expertise. This technological shift arrives alongside what may become the most severe mental health crisis in human history. Our traditional sources of meaning (work, achievement, creativity) are beginning to crumble.

Looking at my two young children, I imagine the world they'll inherit—a world where artificial intelligence fundamentally reshapes what it means to be human. What tools will they need to navigate this unprecedented landscape? How will they find meaning when machines can outperform humans in nearly every domain? These questions make our mission more urgent than ever.

This book emerges from both crisis and possibility. It builds on MBSR's proven foundation while reimagining how mindfulness should be taught, practiced, and managed in our modern world. Through Open MBSR, we're creating deliberate safeguards and fostering genuine dialogue to build institutions that empower rather than subjugate. This isn't about replacing one system with another—it's about transforming hastily assembled scaffolding into a thoughtful, principles-based foundation.

For those of us who have dedicated our careers to sharing these practices, who have witnessed both their transformative potential and their current limitations, this is our moment to create lasting change. Together we can build a movement worthy of the challenges ahead—one that truly empowers individuals to navigate both the current mental health crisis and the profound questions of purpose and meaning that artificial intelligence forces us to confront.

This is an invitation to join in reimagining what mindfulness can be in a world of profound change—to build a movement that truly serves humanity as we navigate the unprecedented challenges ahead.

Introduction

The mindfulness movement stands at a critical juncture. What began as a revolutionary approach to human suffering has become both wildly successful and deeply compromised. As mindfulness programs proliferate in healthcare, education, and corporate settings, fundamental issues threaten to undermine their transformative potential. The rapid mainstreaming of mindfulness has created new forms of spiritual materialism, hidden power structures, and subtle forms of exploitation. Yet within these challenges lies an opportunity for evolution.

This book charts a bold course through the landscape of modern mindfulness, structured in three distinct parts. Part I establishes essential foundations, exploring what mindfulness truly is and examining the revolutionary program that brought it into mainstream consciousness. Part II then confronts the shadow side of contemporary mindfulness, exposing fundamental problems that threaten its transformative potential. Finally, Part III presents Open MBSR—a radical reimagining of how mindfulness can be taught, practiced, and evolved in our rapidly changing world.

Who This Book Is For

This book speaks primarily to mindfulness professionals who have dedicated their lives to this important transformative work. Teachers and facilitators will find new approaches to evolve their practice. Researchers and academics can explore emerging directions in secular mindfulness. Institutional leaders will discover frameworks for making mindfulness more accessible and effective. For internal champions of mindfulness, whether in HR, leadership development, or organizational wellness, these pages offer crucial insights for implementing sustainable, ethically grounded programs.

Why This Book Now

After over a decade of running Mindful Leader and working with thousands of practitioners across dozens of countries, I've witnessed both the profound impact of mindfulness and the systemic issues that limit its potential. The effectiveness of MBSR is clear; I've seen its transformative power firsthand with my organization, teaching hundreds of MBSR classes to thousands of participants. Yet as the largest provider of MBSR training internationally, I've also observed concerning patterns in how these practices are taught and shared.

Despite good intentions, current approaches often create dependency rather than liberation, concentrate power rather than distribute it, and oversimplify rather than embrace complexity. These issues demand more than minor adjustments. They require fundamental reimagining.

My Perspective

My path to this work wasn't linear. With a background in computer engineering and years working in technology and consulting, I bring analytical rigor and practical business experience to these challenges. But my perspective has also been deeply shaped by extensive involvement in contemplative communities. Having served on the board of one of America's largest Buddhist organizations, as well as nonprofits bringing mindfulness to schools and prisons, I've witnessed mindfulness's potential and pitfalls from multiple angles.

As founder and CEO of Mindful Leader, I've straddled the worlds of contemplative practice and organizational transformation. Through launching the Mindful Leadership Summit, certifying over 550 workplace mindfulness facilitators, and creating global practice communities like Meditate Together, I've gained unique insights into what works, what doesn't, and what needs to change.

The insights in this book don't come from theoretical exploration alone. They emerge from years of direct engagement with teachers, practitioners, researchers, and organizations working to bring mindfulness into diverse settings. They reflect both successes and failures, breakthroughs and setbacks. Most importantly, they come from a place of deep respect for MBSR's revolutionary impact coupled with clear-eyed recognition of where evolution is needed.

How to Use This Book

While the book follows a clear progression, different readers may want to engage with it in different ways. Those new to mindfulness might want to start with Part I, building a solid foundation in key concepts and practices. Experienced practitioners might dive directly into Part II's critical analysis. Those ready for immediate change could begin with Part III's practical frameworks.

Throughout the book, you'll find:

- Key takeaways summarizing essential points
- Reflection questions for deeper engagement
- Critical analysis of current approaches
- Practical suggestions for implementation

The Path Forward

The evolution of mindfulness isn't just possible; it's essential. As artificial intelligence reshapes society, as mental health challenges multiply, as traditional institutions struggle to meet modern needs, we need mindfulness practices that are both deeply transformative and truly accessible. This book offers a pathway toward that future.

The journey ahead requires both courage and humility: courage to question established approaches, to confront uncomfortable truths, to imagine new possibilities; humility to examine our blind spots, acknowledge what we don't know, to learn from diverse perspectives, to remain open to continuous evolution.

You're invited to engage with these ideas critically, to question assumptions (including mine), and to contribute your own insights to this emerging framework. The future of mindfulness will be shaped not by any single voice but by our collective wisdom and commitment to genuine transformation.

Let's begin.

Part I

A Starting Point

Imagine a world where the transformative power of mindfulness is accessible to all, free from the influence of hidden agendas, political ideologies, and the commercialization of spirituality. *Open MBSR* presents a groundbreaking, community-centric framework aimed at turning this vision into reality, empowering individuals from all walks of life to cultivate present-moment awareness, resilience, and well-being. Building upon the pioneering work of *Mindfulness-Based Stress Reduction,* or MBSR, this book endeavors to revolutionize how well-being is approached by bringing the life-changing potential of secular mindfulness to the masses. The discussion in Part I explores the foundational aspects of mindfulness and MBSR.

This book speaks primarily to mindfulness professionals who have dedicated their lives to this important transformative work. Teachers and facilitators will find new approaches to evolve their work. Researchers and academics can explore emerging directions in secular mindfulness. Institutional leaders will discover frameworks for making mindfulness more accessible and effective. For internal champions of mindfulness—whether in HR, leadership development, or organizational wellness—these pages offer crucial insights for implementing sustainable, ethically grounded programs. Whether you're encountering these ideas for the first time or have decades of experience, these pages offer both practical insights and a blueprint for transformation.

The journey ahead explores both mindfulness as a universal human capacity and MBSR as its most influential structured program. This dual focus is intentional—understanding the relationship between broad mindfulness practice and specific programs becomes crucial as we build toward a framework that aims to preserve what works while addressing fundamental challenges.

Part I lays this foundation through four chapters:

- Chapter 1 lays the groundwork by describing what mindfulness, meditation, and mindfulness meditation are—and just as importantly, what they are not.
- Chapter 2 provides a deeply defined and wide-ranging examination of MBSR, including its historical development, and describes its profound impact across healthcare, education, the workplace, and even everyday life.
- Chapter 3 delves into MBSR's Buddhist roots—an inevitably imperative discussion if you are to understand how secular mindfulness may peacefully exist and operate in today's complicated world independent of theism.
- Finally, Chapter 4 foreshadows this transformative journey into Open MBSR, through an intriguing exploration of ancient and contemporary cultural, philosophical, and scientific influences.

Chapter 1

The Basics

In the relentless chaos of modern life, a quiet revolution is unfolding. It doesn't promise instant enlightenment or effortless transformation. Instead, it offers something far more valuable: a way to reclaim your mind from the tyranny of distraction and reactivity.

This revolution is mindfulness, and it's not reserved for Zen masters or Silicon Valley gurus. It's a fundamental human capacity that lies dormant within each of us, waiting to be awakened.

But make no mistake. This isn't another self-help fad or productivity hack. It's a radical shift in how we relate to our own minds, our experiences, and the world around us. It's about cultivating a skill that many overlook: the capacity to be fully present, moment by moment, with openness and curiosity instead of judgment or resistance.

In this chapter, I strip away the mysticism and misconceptions surrounding mindfulness and meditation. I dive deep into what these practices really are, how they work, and why they matter. I confront the myths that have held people back and explore the scientific evidence that's propelling mindfulness into the mainstream.

You'll discover that mindfulness isn't about achieving a particular state of mind or escaping reality. It's about seeing reality more clearly, with all its beauty and brutality, and developing the discipline and resilience to engage with it fully.

This chapter grapples with the paradoxes and challenges of mindfulness practice. It explores how something so simple can be so profound, why the very language used to describe mindfulness can sometimes obscure its true nature, and in so doing, I lay the groundwork for a full and comprehensive understanding of the power of MBSR. For many mindfulness professionals reading this book, the foundations covered in this chapter may be familiar ground. Consider it a refresh, or a clarification of shared language, terminology, and approach to the basics before I dive into more complex explorations.

What Is Mindfulness?

At its essence, mindfulness is about reclaiming control of your most precious resource: your attention. It's the mental equivalent of switching from autopilot to manual control but with a crucial twist. Mindfulness isn't just about being present; it's about *how* you're present. It's about approaching your thoughts, feelings, and sensations with an attitude of openness, curiosity, acceptance, and resilience.

Think of it as developing an extraordinary skill: the ability to observe the contents of your consciousness without being swept away by them. This nonjudgmental awareness allows you to engage more fully with your experiences, whether they're pleasant, unpleasant, or neutral.

Cast your mind back to a moment when you were completely absorbed in the present. Perhaps you were watching a sunset paint the sky in vibrant hues or deeply engrossed in a conversation with a close friend that made time stand still. That's a taste of what mindfulness cultivates. It's not about achieving some particular state of mind but about forging a new relationship with your experiences. By cultivating a potent capacity for present-moment awareness, you can open the door to greater clarity, resilience, and well-being.

But there's more to it than just my take. Let's examine what the experts have to say.

Jon Kabat-Zinn (1994), the pioneer who brought mindfulness into the mainstream of Western medicine, defines it as "the awareness that arises from paying attention, on purpose, in the present moment, and nonjudgmentally." Notice the key elements: intentionality, present-moment focus, and acceptance.

Ellen Langer (2014), a Harvard psychology professor who has spent decades studying mindfulness, describes it as "a flexible state of mind in which we are actively engaged in the present, noticing new things and sensitive to context." Langer emphasizes the active engaged nature of mindfulness. It's not about zoning out but about tuning in with heightened awareness.

In recent years, researchers have distinguished between two types of mindfulness:

- **State mindfulness:** The temporary experience of being fully present and aware. Think of it like turning on a spotlight of attention, illuminating the present moment with crystal clarity.
- **Trait mindfulness:** More akin to a character trait; an individual's general tendency to be mindful in daily life. People immersed in trait mindfulness tend to be more consistently aware and less reactive across different situations.

State mindfulness can be induced through brief, focused practices, like adjusting a camera lens to bring a specific object into sharp focus. It's immediate but temporary. Trait mindfulness, on the other hand, develops through habitual practice over time—more like strengthening your overall vision, allowing you to see more clearly in various situations throughout your day.

Drawing all these threads together, we can define mindfulness as our innate ability to pay attention to the present moment with openness, curiosity, and acceptance. It involves maintaining a nonjudgmental awareness of thoughts, emotions, and sensations as they arise, moment by moment. This capacity can be experienced as a temporary state during a brief mindfulness practice, but it can be developed into a more enduring positive trait through regular practice.

By understanding mindfulness in this way, you can set the stage for a profound transformation in how you engage with life. I am not just talking about a way to relax or boost productivity. I am talking about a fundamental shift in how you relate to your experiences; a shift that can transform your well-being, resilience, and personal growth.

The next time someone asks you, "What is mindfulness?" you'll have more than just a clear, comprehensive answer. You'll come to realize that mindfulness isn't merely an idea to grasp; it's a practice to embody and a way of living to nurture every day. With a clear understanding of mindfulness, let's now turn our attention to its close companion: meditation.

What Is Meditation?

Mindfulness and meditation are often conflated, and for an obvious reason—they're intimately intertwined. But to truly harness their potential, you need to understand how they're distinct and how they work in harmony.

> **Note:** Imagine mindfulness as a skill, an ability of the mind, whereas meditation is the training ground, the arena where one forges this power.

But what exactly is meditation? The definitions are myriad. Meditation is often perceived as a singular practice, but it encompasses a vast array of techniques, traditions, and purposes. To truly grasp its scope, it's important to understand that meditation is not limited to one approach or one goal; it is as diverse as the cultures and philosophies that have cultivated it.

Meditation is the intentional practice of training the mind, cultivating mental clarity, emotional resilience, or spiritual growth. It can involve observation, concentration, or active engagement, depending on the technique. The methods vary, but at its heart meditation invites a deliberate shift in how people relate to their thoughts, emotions, and experiences. To expand our understanding, consider the following common types of meditation:

- **Awareness of breath:** Observing the natural rhythm and sensations of breathing as an anchor for present-moment awareness

- **Focused attention (FA):** A trauma-sensitive adaptation of the Awareness of Breath practice, allowing focusing on sounds or touch points.
- **Body scan:** A systematic practice of bringing attention to different parts of the body
- **Open awareness (OA):** Observing the flow of thoughts, emotions, and sensations without attachment or judgment
- **Loving-kindness meditation (Metta):** Actively generating feelings of compassion and goodwill for oneself and others
- **Mantra meditation:** Repeating a sound, word, or phrase to induce meditative awareness
- **Visualization:** Using mental imagery to evoke states or outcomes
- **Movement-based practices:** Techniques such as yoga, Tai Chi, or walking meditation that integrate physical activity with meditative awareness

Meditation's versatility allows it to serve diverse purposes. For some, it is a deeply spiritual practice rooted in traditions like Buddhism or Hinduism, aimed at achieving enlightenment or self-transcendence. For others, it is a secular tool for managing stress, improving focus, or enhancing emotional well-being. It's a practice as ancient as humanity itself, yet as relevant as ever in our modern, technology-driven, distraction-filled world.

It serves two distinct purposes that often create confusion. On the one hand, it's a spiritual practice used for centuries in religious traditions. On the other, it's a secular technique for stress reduction and mental well-being. In this way, meditation is a highly versatile practice, capable of serving both spiritual growth and practical well-being. And it is this dual nature that can create confusion, especially when trying to introduce meditation in nonreligious settings.

Now, how does meditation relate to mindfulness? They're distinct, but they work together in perfect synergy. Mindfulness is the ability to be present with our experience with openness and curiosity. Meditation is one of the most powerful ways to strengthen this capacity.

In the context of mindfulness-based practices, meditation serves as a training ground. It's where you practice bringing your attention to the present moment over and over again. This repetition builds your "mindfulness muscle," making it easier to stay present and aware in your daily life.

As you move forward in exploring mindfulness meditation, this understanding of meditation, in all its diversity and depth, will help you develop programs and practices that serve people across different contexts and settings. Having explored mindfulness and meditation separately, it's time to see how these two powerful concepts come together into mindfulness meditation.

What Is Mindfulness Meditation?

At its core, mindfulness meditation is about training your attention to be fully engaged in the present moment.

The practice is deceptively simple:

1. Choose an anchor for your attention, your rate of breathing, sensations in your body, sounds around you, or a simple phrase.
2. Focus your attention on this anchor with unwavering commitment.
3. When your mind inevitably wanders (and it will; that's part of being human), gently guide your attention back to the anchor without frustration or judgment.
4. Repeat this process, over and over again, with the patience and persistence of a master craftsman honing their skills.

But don't be fooled by this simplicity. The real potency of mindfulness meditation isn't in maintaining a perfectly focused mind. It's in the process of noticing when your mind has wandered and guiding it back. Each time you do this, you're strengthening your "mindfulness muscle," developing a capacity for awareness that will serve you in every aspect of your life.

As you delve deeper into this practice, you might experience moments of profound insight or transformative realizations. You might also encounter periods of agitation and unrest. The beauty of mindfulness meditation is that you're not chasing after peace or transformation. The aim is simply to be aware of your present-moment experience, whatever it may be.

In this non-striving awareness, unexpected insights often emerge. The practice has a way of revealing subtle aspects of your experience; a process that can feel like a gradual unfolding of reality itself. This revealing of nuances in your inner landscape is an intriguing and often unpredictable consequence of consistent practice.

But with that said, it needs to be understood that mindfulness meditation isn't for the faint of heart. It's a practice that challenges you to confront the full spectrum of your experience, from the blissful to the uncomfortable. The key is to find the sweet spot: a practice that meets you where you are while gently pushing the boundaries of your comfort zone.

This approach involves gradual progression, slowly extending your capacity to sit with discomfort, whether physical, mental, or emotional. You might start with shorter, more manageable sessions, then gradually increase duration and intensity as your practice deepens. The goal is to consistently challenge yourself without becoming overwhelmed.

An important distinction of mindfulness meditation is its inherent safeguards against manipulation and abuse. Unlike practices that involve guided imagery, emotional evocation, or the pursuit of altered states, mindfulness meditation's simple focus on observing what's already present, without trying to change or create particular experiences, naturally limits opportunities for psychological manipulation or trauma activation. The teacher's role is simply to explain the technique, not to guide experiences or interpret their meaning. This structural simplicity, combined with its emphasis on developing independent practice skills, helps protect against unhealthy power dynamics and makes it particularly well-suited for secular contexts where maintaining clear boundaries is essential.

Now that you understand the essence of mindfulness meditation, the next sections clarify how different meditation practices relate to it.

Common Anchors for Mindfulness Practice

- Breath
- Body sensations (as in body scan)
- Physical movement
- Sound
- Mantra or phrase
- Visual object or image

Mindfulness Approach

- Present-moment awareness of the chosen anchor
- Noticing and returning when attention wanders
- Nonjudgmental observation of experience
- Acceptance of whatever arises

Non-mindfulness Meditative Approaches

- Absorption in the object to transcend ordinary awareness
- Generation of specific mental or emotional states
- Achievement of particular altered states
- Creative visualization for specific outcomes

> **Note:** Many meditation techniques can be practiced in different ways. For example, focusing on a mantra can be done mindfully using the mantra as an anchor (maintaining awareness of the

> experience moment by moment, including when the mind wanders) or as a means to reach particular states of consciousness (as in Transcendental Meditation, where the mantra is used to settle the mind into progressively quieter states). The distinction lies in the intention and approach to the practice.

Through consistent practice, you learn not just to reduce stress but to cultivate a fundamentally different way of being in the world, one characterized by greater awareness, acceptance, and resilience. Now that you've grasped what mindfulness meditation is, it's equally important to understand what it is *not*. I dispel some common myths and misconceptions in the next section.

What Mindfulness Meditation Is Not

In the cacophony of self-help advice and wellness trends, mindfulness meditation stands out as a beacon of hope for many. But like any powerful tool, it's often misunderstood, shrouded in myths that can lead you astray. It's time to clear the air and confront these misconceptions head-on. Only by stripping away the layers of misunderstanding can you approach this practice with clear eyes and realistic expectations.

Myth #1: The Bliss Delusion

You've felt it, haven't you? That frustration when you sit down to meditate, expecting instant nirvana, only to find your mind racing like a runaway train. This expectation of constant calm is perhaps the most pervasive and damaging myth about mindfulness meditation. The truth? Meditation isn't about floating on a cloud of Zen. It's about cultivating awareness of your present-moment experience, whether that experience is blissful, boring, or downright uncomfortable. The real power lies not in feeling good all the time but in developing the capacity to be present with whatever arises, pleasant or unpleasant.

Myth #2: The Escape Artist's Fantasy

Contrary to popular belief, mindfulness meditation isn't an escape hatch from reality. It's not about achieving some higher state of consciousness or disconnecting from the world. In fact, it's the exact opposite. Mindfulness is about plugging in more deeply to your moment-to-moment experience. It's high-definition living, not checking out but tuning in with razor-sharp clarity to the raw, unfiltered reality of your life.

Myth #3: The Spiritual Straitjacket

While mindfulness has roots in Buddhist traditions, the practice itself is not inherently religious. It's a practical, secular tool for cultivating awareness and well-being. Think of it as mental fitness, no spiritual beliefs required. This misconception often keeps people from exploring mindfulness, fearing it might conflict with their own beliefs or lack thereof. But mindfulness is as secular as physical exercise, a tool available to anyone, regardless of their spiritual, religious, or philosophical leanings.

Myth #4: The Thought-Stopping Fallacy

If you've ever tried to forcibly stop your thoughts, you know it's like trying to hold back a tidal wave with your bare hands. It's not only impossible, but it's also missing the point entirely. Mindfulness meditation isn't about achieving a blank mind. It's about developing a new relationship with your thoughts; observing them without getting swept away in their current.

> **Note:** The goal isn't to stop thoughts but to stop being pushed around by them. It's about freedom from the tyranny of your own mind, not the absence of mental activity.

Myth #5: The Quick-Fix Fantasy

In our culture of instant gratification, it's tempting to see mindfulness meditation as a magic pill that will instantly solve all of life's problems. But meditation is more like exercise for your mind; it requires consistent practice to see results. While it can lead to significant improvements in well-being, it's not an overnight solution to all of life's challenges. The real benefits come from consistent, long-term practice, not from sporadic attempts at finding instant peace.

Why does debunking these myths matter? Because clarity is power. When you strip away the hype and misconceptions, you can approach mindfulness with open eyes and realistic expectations. You are less likely to give up when things don't match these fantasies. You can appreciate the real, often subtle ways mindfulness enhances your life. You're free to approach each meditation with a beginner's mind, one with that sense of openness and curiosity that makes learning so engaging.

Most importantly, understanding what mindfulness isn't helps you see it for what it truly is: a powerful tool for developing awareness, resilience, and a fresh perspective on your experiences. It's not about achieving some idealized monk-like state, but about cultivating a habit that fits into your daily routines and supports you through life's challenges.

Remember, there's no such thing as a "perfect" meditation. Chasing perfection is a surefire way to miss the point entirely. The real goal? Show up. Pay attention. And whatever arises in your mind or during your day, approach it with openness and curiosity. Repeat, over and over again. That's where the true power of mindfulness lies; not in some blissed-out state, but in those small moments of awareness and acceptance.

Another challenge in the world of mindfulness is the problem of language and terminology. I discuss that next.

The Language Paradox

In the ever-expanding universe of mindfulness, we face a crisis of language. As I've delved into the realms of mindfulness, meditation, and their intersection, one truth has emerged with startling clarity: Many people are lost in a fog of their own making. The very words used to describe these transformative practices have become a tangled web of confusion and ambiguity.

This isn't mere semantic quibbling. It's a fundamental flaw that threatens to undermine the entire edifice of mindfulness practice and research. Imagine trying to build a skyscraper on quicksand; that's the precarious state of mindfulness terminology today.

The word "mindfulness" itself has become what linguists call "skunked," meaning a term so overused and misapplied that it's lost its original potency. It's been stretched to cover everything from deep meditative practices to the simple act of savoring a meal. This linguistic bloat isn't just confusing—it's dangerous.

Think about it. How can we hope to harness the transformative power of mindfulness when we can't even agree on what it means? This terminological chaos ripples out, creating real-world consequences:

- It erects barriers to entry, turning what should be an accessible practice into an esoteric, even elitist, maze.
- It hamstrings research efforts. How can we measure and study something we can't define?
- It hinders effective application across diverse settings. Without a common language, how can we integrate these practices into schools, workplaces, and healthcare systems?
- Perhaps most damaging, it undermines the credibility of the entire field. In the absence of clear definitions, charlatans and snake oil salesmen rush in to fill the void.

The stakes couldn't be higher. Without a stable foundation in the terminology, we risk stunting the growth, accessibility, and impact of these powerful practices. We're at a pivotal moment in the field of mindfulness. By establishing common terminology, we have the opportunity to transform it from a fragmented field with disparate approaches and discrete silos into a cohesive discipline with shared language and broad understanding. This unification could amplify mindfulness's impact, uniting teachers, practitioners, and institutions and making it a more influential force in society.

So how do we cut through this Gordian knot of language? How do we "unskunk" mindfulness? The answer lies in a committed effort to clarity and consistency in our language. This isn't just about pedantry; it's about creating a shared foundation that can support the weight of a global movement.

A common language fosters collaboration, breaking down silos and enabling cross-pollination of ideas. It's an open invitation for more people to engage with these practices, tearing down the walls of exclusivity. It provides fertile soil for innovation, allowing the field to grow and evolve while staying rooted in core principles. Most importantly, it creates a shared space where everyone can contribute and grow, fostering a truly inclusive community.

But just as we recognize the urgent need for linguistic clarity, we must also confront a profound paradox at the heart of mindfulness practice. Language is crucial for understanding and sharing mindfulness concepts. It's the map that guides us through our inner landscape. But this map, while useful, is not the territory itself.

> **Note:** Language is the map that guides us through our inner landscape. But this map, although useful, is not the territory itself.

This insight, first articulated by Polish American philosopher Alfred Korzybski (1933) and later applied to mindfulness by Jon Kabat-Zinn, reminds us that our words and concepts about mindfulness are abstractions: useful tools but not the direct experience itself. It's a sobering reminder of both the power and limitations of language in our quest for greater awareness and well-being.

This paradox demands a delicate balancing act. On the one hand, we need clear, well-defined language to effectively teach and discuss mindfulness. On the other, we must remain acutely aware that this language is always an approximation, never the full reality of direct experience.

The challenge before us is to embrace this tension, to strive for clear definitions and frameworks while simultaneously acknowledging their inherent limitations. This balanced approach allows us to create an inclusive, adaptable program that can integrate diverse perspectives while maintaining coherence.

The dance between language and direct experience is where the true transformative potential of mindfulness lies. It invites us to explore the boundaries of what we can describe while remaining open to the vast, uncharted territories or regions of our minds.

As you continue your exploration of mindfulness, hold this paradox with care and curiosity. By recognizing the value and limitations of these linguistic maps, you can cultivate a more nuanced, effective approach to mindfulness practice and teaching.

Remember, the goal isn't to create a perfect linguistic map of mindfulness. It's to use language as a springboard into direct experience. The words are the finger-pointing at the moon, not the moon itself. With a clearer understanding of mindfulness, meditation, and the challenges in discussing them, you can now turn to what science has to say about the benefits of these practices.

What Science Reveals

Mindfulness meditation is not just another wellness fad. It's a practice rooted in ancient wisdom, now validated by cutting-edge neuroscience and psychology research. For those who demand more than anecdotes and feel-good platitudes, let's dive into the hard evidence of what mindfulness meditation can actually do for you.

Stress Reduction: Your Personal Chill Pill

Imagine having a tool that could dial down your stress levels on demand. That's exactly what Khoury and colleagues (2015) found in their 2015 meta-analysis of 29 studies involving over 2,600 participants. The verdict? Mindfulness-based interventions significantly reduced stress, anxiety, and depression in clinical and everyday populations.

- **Emotional regulation: becoming the eye of the storm:** Ever wish you could respond to life's curveballs with more grace? Goldin and Gross (2010) studied individuals with social anxiety disorder. After mindfulness training, participants showed improved emotion regulation, less negative emotion, and increased self-esteem. It's like upgrading your emotional operating system, giving you the power to navigate life's storms with more calm.
- **Laser-like focus: sharpening your mental edge:** In our distraction-filled world, the ability to focus often seems to require nothing short of a superpower. And mindfulness meditation can help you develop it. Jha and colleagues (2007) found that mindfulness training enhanced attention and working memory. Imagine bringing a higher level of laser-like focus to your work, your relationships, and your entire life!
- **Immune boost: training your internal army:** Now, brace yourself for a twist that might challenge everything you thought you knew about the mind–body connection. Davidson et al. (2003) found that an eight-week mindfulness program increased antibody production in response to a flu vaccine. That's right: Mindfulness meditation might actually boost your immune system. It's as if the simple act of paying attention gives your body's natural defenses a pep talk.
- **Pain relief: changing your relationship with discomfort:** For those grappling with chronic pain, mindfulness offers a ray of hope. Hilton et al. (2017) analyzed 38 studies with over 3,500 participants. They found that mindfulness meditation was associated with reductions in chronic pain intensity and improved quality of life. It's not about eliminating pain, but about fundamentally changing your relationship with discomfort.

These findings aren't just interesting trivia to trot out at dinner parties. They're a compelling argument for making mindfulness meditation a cornerstone of your daily life and broader social systems. Imagine the seismic shifts we could create by bringing these benefits into healthcare, education, and workplaces.

But as we stand on the brink of this mindfulness revolution, we must also confront the challenges and criticisms that come with any paradigm shift. The landscape of meditation research is rapidly evolving, constantly challenging our assumptions and opening new possibilities.

Further Exploration

Across leading research institutions, scientists are pushing the boundaries of our understanding of mindfulness meditation:

- Dr. Richard Davidson at the University of Wisconsin-Madison is investigating the neural mechanisms of different meditation practices, potentially leading to more targeted interventions.
- At Harvard Medical School, Dr. Sara Lazar's longitudinal studies on long-term practitioners hint at profound insights into brain plasticity and behavior change.
- Dr. Judson Brewer at Brown University is exploring personalized mindfulness techniques for breaking bad habits.
- Dr. Amishi Jha's research suggests mindfulness could revolutionize performance optimization and stress management under pressure.

These diverse research directions offer tantalizing glimpses of mindfulness's vast potential. In this dynamic field, today's cutting-edge discovery may be tomorrow's foundational practice.

But wait, what about publication bias? As with any field on the cutting edge, we must remain vigilant and self-critical. Voices of dissent offer crucial insights that challenge us to refine our approach and deepen our understanding:

- Dr. Miguel Farias and Dr. Catherine Wikholm (2015), authors of *The Buddha Pill,* raise concerns about overstated benefits and methodological weaknesses in mindfulness research.
- Dr. Willoughby Britton's exploration of adverse effects in meditation practice sheds light on an often-overlooked aspect of mindfulness (Britton et al., 2021).
- The critiques of "McMindfulness" by Dr. David Forbes (2019) and Dr. Ronald Purser (2019) challenge us to examine the broader societal implications of mindfulness practice.
- Dr. Nicholas Van Dam's work highlights fundamental challenges in defining and measuring mindfulness, reminding us of the complexity inherent in studying subjective experiences (Van Dam et al., 2018).

These critical perspectives aren't threats to be silenced. They're essential catalysts for the healthy development of this field, pushing practitioners to elevate their standards, broaden their inquiries, and engage more deeply with the ethical and philosophical dimensions of mindfulness practice.

As I wrap up this exploration of mindfulness and its scientific backing, take a moment to reflect on what you've learned and consider the path forward.

Awakening Your Innate Capacity

In the relentless chaos of the modern world, we've uncovered a beacon of hope. It's not some newfangled technology or miracle drug. It's a fundamental human capacity that's been lying dormant within us all along: mindfulness.

This chapter has peeled back the layers of mysticism and misunderstanding, revealing mindfulness for what it truly is: not some esoteric state reserved for monks and gurus, but a skill we can all develop and strengthen. It's like discovering a hidden innate power, one that's been waiting patiently for us to notice and nurture it.

The chapter has briefly explored meditation not as some woo-woo practice for achieving enlightenment, but as a rigorous training ground where we forge our mindfulness skills. By explaining the symbiosis between mindfulness and meditation, I've laid bare the transformative potential of mindfulness meditation.

Along the way, I've exposed the myths that have long shrouded these practices. Mindfulness isn't about floating on a cloud of bliss or emptying your mind like some human hard drive. It's about developing a radically new relationship with your thoughts and experiences, whatever they may be. It's about sliding out of the passenger seat of your own mind and taking the wheel.

This chapter has grappled with the paradox of language in mindfulness practice. The phrase "the map is not the territory" serves as a potent reminder: while clear terminology is crucial, we must never mistake our descriptions of mindfulness for the raw, unfiltered experience itself.

The deep dive into the scientific evidence supporting mindfulness practices isn't just academic posturing. It's a compelling call to arms, a rallying cry for integrating these practices into every facet of our lives. Yet the chapter also raised the voices of dissent, recognizing that critical perspectives are the whetstone upon which we sharpen our understanding and refine our approach.

Key Takeaways

- Mindfulness is our innate capacity for present-moment awareness, a skill that can be honed through dedicated practice.
- Meditation is a powerful tool for cultivating mindfulness, though not the only path.
- Mindfulness meditation fuses these concepts, training our attention to fully engage with our present-moment experience.

- Scientific research backs various benefits of mindfulness practices, while critical voices help refine our understanding.
- Clear terminology is vital, but we must remember that language can only point toward the direct experience of mindfulness.
- Myths and misconceptions about mindfulness practice can derail our progress, making a clear understanding crucial.

Reflection Questions

1. How has your perception of mindfulness and meditation shifted after this deep dive? What preconceptions have you shed?
2. How might the "map is not the territory" concept reshape your approach to mindfulness practice or teaching?
3. What concrete steps can you take to weave more mindfulness into the fabric of your daily life?

Looking Ahead

Now that you've explored the foundations of mindfulness, meditation, and mindfulness meditation, the next chapter examines the program that brought these practices into mainstream medicine and modern life. Chapter 2 explains how Mindfulness-Based Stress Reduction (MBSR) revolutionized how we understand and practice mindfulness, transforming lives and reshaping societies along the way.

Chapter 2

What Is MBSR?

In 1979, a revolutionary approach to stress management emerged from an unlikely place: a basement office at the University of Massachusetts Medical Center. Jon Kabat-Zinn, a molecular biologist with a deep passion for meditation, had just planted the seeds of what would become a global phenomenon: *Mindfulness-Based Stress Reduction (MBSR)*.

MBSR is more than just a program; it's a paradigm shift in how people approach well-being. It's the bridge between ancient wisdom and modern science, offering a practical, evidence-based path to resilience and inner peace. This isn't about escaping life's challenges, but developing the tools to navigate them with grace and clarity.

The journey into MBSR begins with Jon Kabat-Zinn himself. His story is one of curiosity, innovation, and a relentless pursuit of truth. This chapter explores how his unique blend of scientific rigor and spiritual insight shaped MBSR's development and propelled it onto the world stage.

At its core, MBSR is a carefully crafted curriculum, each element precisely calibrated to cultivate mindfulness and self-awareness. This chapter dissects this curriculum, examining how each component contributes to the whole. The *MBSR Authorized Curriculum Guide and Standards of Practice* (Santorelli et al., 2017) serves as the guardrails, ensuring consistency and quality across MBSR programs worldwide.

But MBSR's impact extends far beyond individual well-being. Today it is reshaping entire industries:

- **Healthcare:** Revolutionizing approaches to chronic pain, stress, and mental health
- **Education:** Fostering emotional intelligence and resilience in students
- **Workplace:** Enhancing productivity, creativity, and employee satisfaction

Central to MBSR's success are its teachers; the torchbearers of mindfulness. This chapter explores the landscape of *MBSR Teacher Training,* uncovering the rigorous pathways available to those called to share this transformative practice. From leading institutions to core competencies, I examine what it takes to become an effective MBSR instructor.

By the end of this exploration, you'll have a comprehensive understanding of MBSR: its origins, practices, and profound implications for the future of well-being. Yet, like any pioneering approach, MBSR isn't without its limitations. As you progress through this book, you'll learn how Open MBSR aims to build on MBSR's solid foundation while addressing some of its challenges.

> **Note:** As you delve into MBSR, pay attention to what resonates with you. Notice the elements that spark your curiosity or challenge your assumptions. These insights will be invaluable as you later examine how Open MBSR seeks to create a more inclusive, ethical, and adaptable approach to mindfulness.

For now, get ready to immerse yourself in the world of MBSR, the program that brought mindfulness out of the monastery and into hospitals, boardrooms, and classrooms around the globe. It's time to uncover the story behind this influential approach and understand why it continues to captivate millions worldwide.

What Is MBSR?

In 1979, Jon Kabat-Zinn unleashed a revolution from the basement of the University of Massachusetts Medical Center. His creation, Mindfulness-Based Stress Reduction (MBSR), would go on to reshape our understanding of mental health and well-being.

MBSR isn't just another self-help fad. It's a rigorous mental training program, as demanding and transformative as any physical regimen. Over eight weeks, participants engage in a combination of mindfulness meditation, gentle yoga, and group dialogue. The goal? To fundamentally alter how they engage with stress, pain, and the complexities of daily life.

This isn't about passive learning. MBSR demands active participation. It's a full-contact sport for the mind, where theory meets practice in real time. Through a series of formal practices, participants develop a new relationship with their thoughts and experiences. They learn to observe without judgment, to respond rather than react.

The MBSR blueprint:

- An eight-week intensive program, featuring weekly 2.5-hour sessions and a full-day retreat
- Formal mindfulness practices: body scans, sitting meditation, walking meditation, and gentle yoga
- Group discussions to deepen understanding and share experiences
- Daily home practice to integrate mindfulness into everyday life
- A focus on experiential learning and practical application
- Emphasis on stress reduction and enhanced quality of life

These practices are guided by the nine attitudes of mindfulness that Kabat-Zinn articulated in his seminal work, *Full Catastrophe Living* (2013): nonjudging, patience, beginner's mind, trust, non-striving, acceptance, letting go, gratitude, and generosity.

These attitudes shape how the practices are taught and experienced throughout the program.

What sets MBSR apart?

- **MBSR's distinctly secular:** Evidence-based approach marries ancient wisdom with modern science, presenting mindfulness in a universal, nonreligious context. It's built on a foundation of rigorous research and medical understanding.
- **An intensive, structured curriculum:** MBSR isn't a quick fix. It's a deep dive into mindfulness, demanding commitment and consistency. Like learning a new language, full immersion is key.
- **Widespread application:** From its origins in chronic pain management, MBSR has found positive application in hospitals, classrooms, and corporate boardrooms. Its adaptability has fueled its global impact.

MBSR challenges participants to reconsider their relationships with their own minds. It asks participants to confront habitual patterns of thought and behavior, to question the stories they tell themselves about who they are and what they're capable of.

As you contemplate MBSR, consider this: How might your life change if you could observe your thoughts and feelings without being controlled by them? What possibilities might open up if you could respond to life's challenges with clarity and compassion, rather than knee-jerk reactions?

The power of MBSR lies not just in its techniques, but in its potential to fundamentally alter your perspective. It offers a new lens through which to view yourself and the world around you. In a society obsessed with external solutions and dubious "life hacks," MBSR dares to suggest that the most profound changes come from within.

Jon Kabat-Zinn and the History of MBSR

In 1944, a child was born in New York City who would go on to revolutionize our understanding of the mind. Jon Kabat-Zinn, the son of a molecular immunologist and a painter, embodied from birth the fusion of scientific rigor and creative insight that would later define his life's work.

Kabat-Zinn's early path seemed conventional enough. He excelled in chemistry at Haverford College and dove into molecular biology at MIT. But in 1966, fate intervened. A talk by Zen missionary Philip Kapleau ignited a spark in Kabat-Zinn that would ultimately set the world ablaze.

Suddenly, meditation wasn't just an esoteric, mystery-laden Eastern practice. It was a calling, a potential key to unlocking human potential. Kabat-Zinn immersed himself in Zen and Vipassana meditation, studying under luminaries like Thích Nhất Hạnh and Seung Sahn. These weren't mere spiritual dalliances. Rather, they became the building blocks of a revolutionary vision: mindfulness as a universal practice, adaptable to modern Western society.

In 1979, this vision crystallized into the Stress Reduction Clinic at the University of Massachusetts Medical Center. Here, Kabat-Zinn forged what would later become MBSR, an eight-week course that would change the face of mental health.

MBSR was more than just another wellness program. It was a Rosetta Stone, translating ancient wisdom into the language of Western medicine and psychology. It focused on experiential learning, not esoteric teachings. It made mindfulness accessible to everyone, not just to spiritual seekers.

As MBSR gained traction, Kabat-Zinn became its tireless advocate. His books, like *Full Catastrophe Living* and *Wherever You Go, There You Are,* brought mindfulness to the masses. His scientific background lent credibility. His charisma made it irresistible.

The evolution of MBSR:

1979: Kabat-Zinn establishes the Stress Reduction Clinic at UMass Medical Center with a stress reduction program.

1990: The publication of *Full Catastrophe Living* brings the principles of mindfulness and stress reduction to a wider audience.

1993: Bill Moyers's PBS series "Healing and the Mind" introduces MBSR to mainstream America.

1995: UMass Center for Mindfulness established at UMass Medical School to advance MBSR research and training.

2000s: A growing body of research validates MBSR's effectiveness across multiple domains.

2010s: MBSR becomes widely adopted in healthcare, education, and corporate settings.

Kabat-Zinn's approach, a potent blend of science, Buddhist wisdom, and social consciousness, didn't just create a program. It sparked a paradigm shift in how we approach well-being and resilience.

MBSR stands as a testament to the power of bridging worlds. It's the connective tissue between ancient wisdom and cutting-edge science, a tool for navigating life's storms with grace and clarity.

> **Note:** As you reflect on Kabat-Zinn's journey, consider this: What overlooked connections in your own life might lead to revolutionary insights? How might blending seemingly disparate fields of knowledge open up new possibilities?

The story of MBSR reminds us that the most profound innovations often arise at the intersection of different disciplines. It challenges us to look beyond our usual boundaries, to seek wisdom in unexpected places. In a world of increasing specialization, MBSR stands as a powerful argument for the value of cross-pollination and holistic thinking.

The Impact of MBSR

MBSR has quietly sparked a revolution in how we approach well-being, its influence extending far beyond the realm of healthcare. Like a stone cast into still waters, it has created ripples that touch every corner of society, from bustling corporate offices to serene classrooms.

The bedrock of MBSR's success is its scientific foundation. Study after study has demonstrated its power to alleviate stress, anxiety, and depression while enhancing overall well-being. As I stressed previously, this isn't some new-age fad; it's hard science. And that's what's caught the attention of doctors, CEOs, and educators alike.

MBSR's unique strength lies in its secular, nondogmatic nature. It offers mindfulness without mysticism, making it accessible to people from all walks of life. It's a universal language of well-being, as easily understood by Silicon Valley executives as by Midwest schoolteachers.

In healthcare, MBSR is rewriting the rulebook. Doctors are increasingly incorporating mindfulness into their treatment plans, offering patients a powerful tool to manage everything from chronic pain to anxiety. It's not just about treating symptoms; it's about empowering patients to become active participants in their own healing journey.

The business world has taken notice. Companies like Google and Intel are embracing mindfulness programs, recognizing their potential to boost employee well-being, productivity, and job satisfaction, and even to enhance creative thinking. It's not just a perk; it's becoming a competitive advantage.

At Mindful Leader, we've been at the vanguard of the workplace mindfulness movement, certifying over 550 workplace mindfulness facilitators. Each of these facilitators completed MBSR as part of their training, underscoring how deeply MBSR has permeated the corporate world.

In education, MBSR is reshaping how we approach learning and personal development. From elementary school classrooms to university lecture halls, mindfulness programs are equipping students with the skills they need to navigate our complex, fast-paced world.

Nonprofits like Inner Explorer are bringing mindfulness to young learners, teaching them how to manage stress, regulate emotions, and cultivate focus. At the university level, MBSR is being woven into curricula ranging from psychology to business, preparing the next generation of leaders to face challenges with skill and compassion.

One of MBSR's most remarkable impacts is the global community it has fostered. Practitioners, researchers, and educators worldwide are united by a shared commitment to the power of mindfulness. This network is driving innovation, sharing best practices, and making mindfulness accessible to all.

The UMass Center for Mindfulness, founded by Jon Kabat-Zinn, has been the epicenter of this movement, training hundreds of MBSR teachers and laying the groundwork for the global mindfulness community. More recently, the Mindfulness Center at Brown University has taken up the MBSR torch, advancing mindfulness research and practice.

At Mindful Leader, we've been instrumental in expanding MBSR's reach, offering hundreds of classes, becoming the largest provider of MBSR training internationally. We recognize MBSR as the cornerstone for understanding mindfulness in secular settings.

As we look to the future, MBSR's impact offers a glimpse of what's possible when we embrace mindfulness as a tool for personal and societal transformation. By building on this legacy, we have the opportunity to create a world where resilience, compassion, and well-being are the norm, not the exception.

The question now is this: How will you contribute to this transformation? What ripples will you create in your own pond of influence?

MBSR Curriculum

At the core of MBSR lies a powerful blueprint: the *Mindfulness-Based Stress Reduction (MBSR) Authorized Curriculum Guide* (2014). Developed by the University of Massachusetts Medical School Center for Mindfulness, this guide serves as the North Star for MBSR teachers worldwide. It's a detailed roadmap charting the course of the eight-week MBSR journey. The guide is a treasure trove, containing:

- Weekly session themes and key components
- Formal and informal mindfulness practices

- Group discussion topics
- Educational content

But it's more than a list of activities. The guide embodies the core principles of MBSR: nonjudgmental awareness, a non-striving attitude, and self-compassion. It's like a master craftsman's handbook, not only providing tools but teaching the art itself.

The MBSR program is an eight-week odyssey, each session lasting 2.5–3.5 hours. It's a mindfulness immersion, complete with an all-day silent retreat between weeks 6 and 7. Each week builds upon the last, layering mindfulness skills like an artisan crafting a masterpiece. The themes are guiding lights, illuminating specific aspects of mindfulness in teachings and discussions. The practices are the building blocks, formal mindfulness techniques that participants engage with in class and at home, including body scans, sitting meditation, yoga, and walking meditation.

Before embarking on this eight-week journey, two crucial steps set the stage:

- **Orientation session:** An introductory meeting where potential participants glimpse the MBSR landscape, experience a taste of mindfulness practice, and decide if they're ready for the journey.
- **Pre-class interview:** A one-on-one meeting with the MBSR instructor, aligning expectations, addressing concerns, and ensuring the participant is prepared for the commitment ahead.

The week-by-week progression is described next.

Week 1: Introduction to Mindfulness

- **Theme:** There is more right with you than wrong with you
- **Practices:** Body scan, mindful eating, awareness of breath
- **Focus:** Beginner's mind and nonjudging

Week 2: Perception and Creative Responding
- **Theme:** How perception influences response
- **Practices:** Body scan, sitting meditation, introduction to yoga
- **Focus:** Automatic pilot and stress reactivity

Week 3: Experiencing the Present Moment
- **Theme:** The pleasure and power of being present
- **Practices:** Sitting meditation (breath, body sensations), yoga, walking meditation
- **Focus:** Embodiment and working with physical limitations

Week 4: Stress: Responding versus Reacting
- **Theme:** Exploring conditioned reactions and mindful responses
- **Practices:** Sitting meditation (breath, body, sounds, thoughts), yoga
- **Focus:** Physiological and psychological bases of stress

Week 5: Allowing and Letting Be
- **Theme:** Cultivating acceptance toward all experiences
- **Practices:** Sitting meditation (open awareness), yoga, walking meditation
- **Focus:** Turning toward difficulties with openness

Week 6: Mindfulness and Communication
- **Theme:** Awareness in interpersonal interactions
- **Practices:** Sitting meditation, yoga, walking meditation
- **Focus:** Mindful listening and speaking

All-Day Silent Retreat

- Extended mindfulness practice (six to seven hours)
- Sequence of sitting, walking, and mindful movement
- Deepening concentration and continuity of mindfulness

Week 7: Integrating Mindfulness into Daily Life

- **Theme:** Incorporating mindfulness into everyday activities
- **Practices:** Sitting meditation, yoga, body scan, walking meditation
- **Focus:** Lifestyle choices and nourishing activities

Week 8: Sustaining the Practice

- **Theme:** Reflecting on insights and maintaining practice
- **Practices:** Body scan, sitting meditation, yoga
- **Focus:** Key learnings and sustaining momentum

Throughout this journey, participants engage in daily home practices. It's like mastering an art in which consistent practice is the key to transformation.

The MBSR curriculum is more than a set of techniques. It's a path of self-discovery, a way to forge a new relationship with stress, pain, and life's challenges. By fully immersing in this curriculum, participants tap into wellsprings of resilience, clarity, and well-being they never knew they possessed.

This is not just learning; it's unlearning. It's not just about adding new skills, but about stripping away layers of conditioning to reveal the innate wisdom and strength that lies within each of us. The MBSR journey is an invitation to reclaim our lives, one mindful moment at a time.

MBSR Standards of Practice and Other Resources

The UMass Center for Mindfulness crafted the *Mindfulness-Based Stress Reduction (MBSR): Standards of Practice* as a companion to their curriculum guide. This document is much more than a simple set of rules: It's a comprehensive framework ensuring MBSR programs worldwide maintain their integrity and potency.

These standards, born from Jon Kabat-Zinn's vision in 1979, have evolved like a living organism, adapting to the changing landscape of mindfulness practice. The most recent iteration, released in 2014, outlines the universal principles that form the bedrock of authentic MBSR teaching.

The *Standards of Practice* are structured around six key pillars:

- MBSR Teacher Readiness and Competency
- Pre-Program Group Orientation Sessions
- Screening Criteria for Exclusion
- Participant/Provider Informal Learning Contract
- Hours of Instruction
- Classroom Instruction: Curriculum Guidelines

Each pillar is a crucial support, ensuring the MBSR experience remains transformative and true to its roots.

But here's the rub: These standards haven't been updated in a decade. The landscape of mindfulness-based interventions has shifted dramatically since then. The Oasis Institute, once the gold standard for MBSR teacher training, is no longer operational. And when important changes are made, like when Jon Kabat-Zinn expanded an element of MBSR called the seven attitudes of mindfulness into the nine attitudes of mindfulness, these changes have not been uniformly disseminated, creating conflicting understandings and teachings.

This leaves us at a crossroads. Should we cling to these aging standards or allow for organic evolution and local adaptation? It's a question that cuts to the heart of MBSR's identity and future.

While the official standards have remained static, the MBSR community hasn't stood still. Influential works like Jon Kabat-Zinn's *Full Catastrophe Living* and Saki Santorelli's *Heal Thy Self* have become unofficial guideposts, shaping the understanding and practice of MBSR worldwide.

Saki Santorelli, in particular, played a pivotal role in the practical, mentorship-driven training of MBSR practitioners. As demand for MBSR teachers skyrocketed, his leadership was instrumental in formalizing and expanding teacher training programs.

Yet, as MBSR has grown, it's also diversified. The program essentially transitioned from UMass to the Mindfulness Center at Brown University in 2020. Other organizations including Mindful Leader, UC San Diego Center for Mindfulness, and the Mindfulness Network in the UK have emerged, each putting their own interpretation on MBSR while still honoring its core principles.

This growth raises a critical question: How do we balance the need for consistency and integrity with the potential benefits of increased accessibility, diversity, and innovation?

Adding another layer of complexity is the issue of ownership. While MBSR was once trademarked by Jon Kabat-Zinn in 2000 to protect its integrity and ensure fidelity to the program's principles, the trademark was later allowed to lapse. I imagine this decision reflects Kabat-Zinn's intention to make MBSR a gift to the world, freely shared and widely adopted. However, this openness has also led to concerns about maintaining quality and consistency, as adaptations and variations of the program continue to emerge globally.

As we stand at this juncture, contemplating the future of MBSR and the potential of Open MBSR, we're faced with a series of challenges and opportunities:

- How do we maintain the core principles of MBSR while allowing for innovation?

- Who has the authority to set and enforce standards in the absence of legal ownership?
- How can individual practitioners and organizations contribute to maintaining quality and effectiveness?
- What are the most critical aspects of MBSR that must be preserved as we move forward?

These aren't academic questions. They strike at the heart of MBSR's identity and its potential to continue transforming lives. As we navigate this terrain, we must remember that the goal isn't just to preserve a program, but to nurture a practice that has the power to alleviate suffering and cultivate wisdom on a global scale.

The path forward isn't clear-cut, yet it's ripe with potential. By building on the solid foundation of the original MBSR while embracing a more inclusive, transparent, and community-driven approach, we have the opportunity to bring the profound benefits of mindfulness to an even wider audience. The question is: Are we ready to rise to this challenge?

MBSR Teacher Training

The journey of MBSR teacher training is a testament to human potential and the power of dedicated practice. It's a path that demands not just knowledge, but embodiment, a living, breathing example of the principles being taught. From its roots in informal apprenticeships to the structured programs of today, this evolution mirrors the growth of MBSR itself.

Key milestones in this journey:

1979: Jon Kabat-Zinn develops MBSR at UMass Medical Center.

1983: Saki Santorelli becomes the first intern in the Stress Reduction Clinic.

1990s: Informal apprenticeship model for teacher training emerges.

2001: Saki Santorelli founds the Oasis Institute, the first school for training MBSR teachers.

2017: Saki Santorelli retires, marking the end of an era.

2018–2019: Brown University essentially takes over UMass teacher training.

2000s–Present: Additional MBSR teacher training programs proliferate worldwide.

The landscape of MBSR teacher training today is highly varied, with programs differing significantly in quality, structure, and philosophical orientation. While institutions like Brown University and the University of California, San Diego, offer well-established pathways, others lean too heavily on Buddhist influences or are led by underqualified teachers. Some programs maintain strong standards but can be overly rigid, while others lack the depth and discipline necessary to ensure competent instruction. Amid this diversity, organizations like Mindful Leader and others worldwide provide alternative approaches, each shaping the next generation of MBSR teachers in its own way.

The core objectives remain constant:

- Provide a deep understanding of the MBSR curriculum
- Foster a sustained personal mindfulness practice
- Develop essential teaching competencies
- Cultivate the embodiment of mindfulness in daily life
- Ensure the delivery of authentic, high-quality MBSR programs

But the path is not without its challenges. The field grapples with issues of standardization, accessibility, and inclusivity. The time and financial commitments required can be substantial. A typical comprehensive program can take two to three years and cost upward of $10,000 US.

The journey often unfolds in stages:

- **Prerequisites:** Completion of an eight-week MBSR course, established daily practice, silent retreats
- **Foundational training:** In-depth curriculum study, personal practice cultivation, basic teaching skills
- **Advanced training:** Supervised teaching, deepening practice, mentorship
- **Certification:** Demonstration of mastery, comprehensive assessment, ongoing development

This path is more than just acquiring skills: It's a profound personal transformation. It demands balancing personal and professional demands while navigating the complexities of bringing an ancient practice into modern life.

As the field evolves, pressing questions emerge. How do we maintain the integrity of MBSR while allowing for innovation? How can we ensure diversity and inclusivity among both teachers and participants? How do we balance the need for standards with the desire for accessibility?

These challenges are not roadblocks, but opportunities. They invite us to embody the very principles we teach: presence, nonjudgment, and compassion. They call us to continually refine and expand our understanding of what it means to be a teacher of mindfulness in today's world.

The future of MBSR teacher training is not set in stone. It's a living, breathing field shaped by each person who steps onto this path. As we move forward, we carry the wisdom of pioneers like Kabat-Zinn and Santorelli, while also creating space for new voices and approaches.

In the end, becoming an MBSR teacher is about more than mastering a curriculum. It's about embarking on a lifelong journey of growth, compassion, and service. It's about becoming a living example of the transformative power of mindfulness. And in doing so, we open the door for countless others to discover their own capacity for presence, resilience, and well-being.

Honoring Roots

This chapter has journeyed through the rich landscape of MBSR. From its humble beginnings in a UMass basement to its global impact today, MBSR has revolutionized our approach to well-being. This chapter explored its core curriculum, the rigorous standards that guide its practice, and the transformative path of teacher training. This isn't just a program; it's a paradigm shift, a bridge between ancient wisdom and modern science that continues to reshape lives, industries, and societies.

MBSR stands as a testament to human potential, not just in its ability to alleviate suffering, but in its power to cultivate profound awareness and compassion. It challenges us to look beyond quick fixes and external solutions, inviting us to tap into the wellspring of resilience and clarity that lies within each of us.

Key Takeaways

- MBSR is a secular, evidence-based approach that makes mindfulness accessible to all.

- The eight-week MBSR curriculum is a carefully crafted journey of self-discovery and transformation.

- MBSR's impact extends far beyond individual well-being, reshaping healthcare, education, and business.

- The *MBSR Standards of Practice* ensure consistency and quality, but face challenges in a rapidly evolving field.

- MBSR teacher training is a rigorous path of personal and professional transformation.

- The future of MBSR lies in balancing integrity with innovation and accessibility with rigorous standards.

- MBSR's lack of legal ownership presents both opportunities and challenges for its future development.

Reflection Questions

1. How might the principles and practices of MBSR be adapted to address emerging global challenges?
2. What role could technology play in expanding MBSR's reach while maintaining the integrity of its core teachings?
3. How can the MBSR community foster greater diversity and inclusivity, both in its teacher base and the populations it serves?

Looking Ahead

The next chapter traces MBSR's Buddhist roots, uncovering how ancient wisdom shaped modern mindfulness. It explores the Three Jewels, the Four Noble Truths, and other key Buddhist concepts that helped inform MBSR's foundation.

Chapter 3
Buddhist Roots of MBSR

Imagine standing at the intersection of ancient wisdom and modern science. This is the birthplace of Mindfulness-Based Stress Reduction (MBSR), a revolutionary approach that blends timeless insights with cutting-edge research. MBSR isn't just another wellness trend; it's a catalyst for transformation, quietly channeling age-old wisdom into the heart of our hyper-modern world.

To truly grasp MBSR's power, we must trace its roots back to the fertile soil of Buddhist philosophy and yogic tradition. This chapter is an expedition into that rich territory, uncovering how the Buddha's teachings have been distilled and refined for our modern minds, while exploring how core practices like breath awareness, body scans, and open awareness emerged from centuries of contemplative tradition.

In this chapter, you learn that the Four Noble Truths, the Eightfold Path, and the Four Foundations of Mindfulness are not just abstract concepts, but rather they are the bedrock upon which MBSR was built. The Buddha's principle of *ehipassiko*, which translates to "come and see for yourself," lives on in MBSR's emphasis on experiential learning.

The Nine Attitudes of Mindfulness developed by Jon Kabat-Zinn, which are explored extensively in MBSR teacher training and his book *Full Catastrophe Living,* aren't mere slogans. They're the fruit of 2,500 years of contemplative practice, adapted for 21st-century lives. I decode these attitudes, revealing their ancient DNA while appreciating their universal relevance.

But MBSR embraces more than sitting still and contemplating. It recognizes the embodied nature of humans, the inextricable link between mind and body. Enter yoga, not as a series of Instagram-worthy poses, but as "mindful yoga," a cornerstone of the MBSR approach.

As you navigate this terrain, you'll confront challenging questions:

- How does MBSR balance its Buddhist heritage with secular, scientific ambitions?
- What's gained, and potentially lost, in this cultural translation?
- How can we honor these wisdom traditions while making mindfulness accessible to all?

The exploration in this chapter lays essential groundwork for Open MBS, an initiative that builds on both MBSR's Buddhist roots and contemporary understanding. By deeply examining these origins and being transparent about their influence, you can develop practices that authentically evolve to meet contemporary needs.

The Origins of Core MBSR Practices

The core practices of MBSR—awareness of breath, body scan, open awareness, and loving-kindness—emerged from Buddhist contemplative traditions refined over centuries. Modern presentations often obscure these origins, creating issues around transparency and authenticity. Understanding the Buddhist roots and how they were adapted for secular contexts is essential for ethical integrity and effective teaching.

The following sections examine each practice in its current MBSR form and trace it back to its contemplative origins.

Awareness of Breath: The Foundation

In MBSR, breath awareness seems simple enough: Focus on your breathing, notice when your mind wanders, and gently return. It's taught as a basic tool for developing present-moment awareness and an anchor for a wandering mind. The instruction is straightforward: Bring attention to the natural sensations of breathing, whether at the nostrils, chest, or abdomen, and keep returning to these sensations whenever attention strays.

The Buddhist original, Ānāpānasati (literally "mindfulness of breathing"), wasn't just a relaxation technique. Detailed in the *Ānāpānasati Sutta,* it was considered a complete path to enlightenment. Monastics spent years refining this practice in isolated settings, viewing it through the lens of Buddhist cosmology and ethics. The practice was embedded in complex frameworks of concentration states (jhānas) and insight development.

MBSR strips away the religious framework while preserving the core methodology. It's like taking a precision instrument and recalibrating it for a new purpose. The fundamental mechanics—systematic attention to breath sensations, methods for handling distraction, and emphasis on direct experience—remain intact. What's removed are the Buddhist metaphysics: references to Karma, enlightenment, and religious terminology.

Body Scan: Mapping Inner Territory

In MBSR, the body scan appears straightforward: systematically moving attention through the body, from toes to head or head to toes. Practitioners rest their awareness on each body part in sequence, noting whatever sensations are present, tingling, pressure, temperature, or even the absence of sensation. It's presented as a foundational practice for developing detailed awareness of physical experience while learning to be with both comfort and discomfort.

The Buddhist origins of this practice reveal a far more ambitious agenda. Detailed in the *Kāyagatāsati Sutta* (Mindfulness of the Body Discourse), the original practice encompassed a comprehensive system of body contemplation. Buddhist practitioners performed not just systematic scanning, but intensive contemplation of anatomical parts, elements, and even decay. They would meditate in charnel grounds, observing decomposing corpses to develop insight into impermanence and nonattachment to physical form.

MBSR preserves the methodical investigation of bodily experience while discarding elements that might alienate modern practitioners. Gone are the cemetery contemplations and emphasis on "disenchantment" with physical form. What remains is a powerful method for developing intimate awareness of present-moment bodily experience, teaching practitioners to relate to physical sensations, including pain and discomfort, with greater awareness and less reactivity.

Open Awareness: The Space of Mind

In MBSR, open awareness involves maintaining a broad, receptive attention to whatever arises in experience. Rather than focusing on a specific object like the breath, practitioners are invited to notice thoughts, emotions, sensations, and sounds as they naturally occur. It's taught as a way to develop greater flexibility of attention and a more spacious relationship with experience, helping people observe mental patterns without getting caught in them.

The Buddhist foundations of this practice span multiple traditions, each offering unique approaches. In Theravada Buddhism's vipassanā traditions, particularly the Mahāsi Sayadaw lineage, practitioners used systematic noting techniques to observe phenomena. Zen Buddhism's Sōtō school developed *shikantaza* ("just sitting"), emphasizing relaxed alertness. Tibetan Buddhism's Dzogchen and Mahamudra traditions offered sophisticated methods like *trekchö* ("cutting through") for resting in the mind's natural state.

MBSR distills these various streams into a secular practice focused on developing flexible attention and a skillful relationship with experience. It's like taking a complex recipe and identifying its essential ingredients, maintaining what works while making it accessible to everyone. The practice preserves the fundamental approach of nonpreferential observation while removing traditional religious frameworks and metaphysical concepts.

Loving-Kindness: The Heart Practice

In MBSR, loving-kindness practice involves cultivating positive intentions and goodwill, first toward oneself and then expanding to others. Practitioners typically use simple phrases like "May I be happy" or "May you be well," while opening to feelings of warmth and care. It's presented as a practical method for developing emotional resilience and healthier relationships with self and others.

Traditional *metta bhavana* (loving-kindness cultivation) was one of Buddhism's four "divine abodes" (Brahmaviharas), alongside compassion, appreciative joy, and equanimity. The practice followed precise methods and formulas, using specific Pali phrases and visualizations. It was viewed as a complete path of spiritual development, aimed at purifying the mind, generating positive Karma, and supporting enlightenment through the progressive expansion of goodwill to all beings.

MBSR's adaptation preserves the systematic cultivation of positive intentions while removing traditional elements that might create barriers for secular practitioners. Gone are the Pali phrases, Buddhist cosmology, and religious imagery. The practice maintains its power for emotional transformation while becoming more accessible to contemporary practitioners of any background or belief system.

This pattern of careful adaptation, preserving essential methods while removing religious and cultural elements, characterizes MBSR's approach to all these practices. It's not about diluting their power but about making them accessible while maintaining transparency about their origins. Understanding this history can help you appreciate both the depth of these practices and the thoughtful way they've been adapted for modern contexts.

The Three Jewels of Buddhism: Buddha, Dhamma, and Sangha

The Three Jewels of Buddhism—Buddha, Dhamma, and Sangha—aren't just ancient relics. They're living principles that have shaped mindfulness practices for millennia, including the modern iteration known as Mindfulness-Based Stress Reduction (MBSR).

These jewels, first articulated in the *Pali Canon's Khuddakapatha*,[1] form the foundation of Buddhist practice:

Buddham saranam gacchami   *I go to the Buddha for refuge*
Dhammam saranam gacchami   *I go to the Dhamma for refuge*
Sangham saranam gacchami"   *I go to the Sangha for refuge.*

While MBSR isn't Buddhism repackaged, these concepts have profoundly influenced its development. They provide a framework for understanding the teacher–student dynamic, the importance of practical teachings, and the role of community in personal growth.

The following sections examine each jewel and its MBSR counterpart.

The Buddha Jewel

In Buddhism, the *Buddha Jewel* represents a dual concept: the historical figure of Siddhartha Gautama[2] and the innate potential for awakening within every individual. MBSR adapts this idea, stripping away its religious connotations. The role of the Buddha is reimagined as the mindfulness teacher, a secular guide rather than a spiritual leader. Simultaneously, MBSR embraces the notion that each participant possesses the inherent capacity to cultivate greater awareness and well-being. This subtle shift maintains the essence of self-discovery and personal growth central to the original concept, while presenting it in a secular, universally accessible format.

The Dhamma Jewel

Buddhism presents the *Dhamma Jewel* as a comprehensive set of teachings, including the Four Noble Truths, the Eightfold Path, and fundamental principles like impermanence. MBSR distills this vast body of wisdom into a practical, secular curriculum. Instead of doctrinal teachings, MBSR offers concrete practices such as mindful breathing, body scans, and yoga. These techniques, while rooted in Buddhist insights, are presented without religious context. The underlying principles of awareness and acceptance in MBSR echo the essence of Buddhist teachings, but are framed in universal, experiential terms. This transformation preserves the transformative power of the original teachings while making them accessible to a diverse, modern audience.

The Sangha Jewel

In Buddhism, the *Sangha Jewel* represents the community of practitioners, serving as a support network and a wellspring of collective wisdom. MBSR reinterprets this concept for a secular context, embodying it in the group dynamic of course participants. The shared journey of MBSR creates a microcosm of the traditional Sangha, where individuals come together to practice, share experiences, and support one another's growth. This communal aspect fosters a sense of belonging and mutual encouragement, mirroring the traditional Sangha's role but without religious overtones. By emphasizing peer support and shared learning, MBSR maintains the essence of community central to Buddhist practice while adapting it to suit a diverse, modern audience seeking stress reduction and personal development.

> **Note:** While MBSR participants don't formally "take refuge" in the Three Jewels as Buddhists do, the program subtly weaves aspects of each into its fabric. The role of the Buddha is reimagined in the mindfulness teacher and each participant's innate capacity for awareness. The Dhamma finds expression in the curriculum's practical techniques and underlying principles. The Sangha manifests in the supportive group dynamic of MBSR courses and community participation.

> It is important to recognize that this integration does not make MBSR Buddhist. Rather, it demonstrates the program's ability to distill timeless wisdom into a contemporary format.

By understanding these influences, you gain insight into MBSR's depth and its skillful adaptation of ancient practices to modern needs. This transformation preserves the essence of Buddhist teachings while creating a secular, accessible approach to mindfulness and stress reduction.

The Four Noble Truths and the Eightfold Path

Much like the Three Jewels of Buddhism, the Four Noble Truths and the Eightfold Path draw upon thousands of years of philosophy. Today they remain vibrant diagnostic tools and treatment plans for the human condition, offering insights that resonate across cultures and millennia.

The Four Noble Truths, first articulated by the Buddha, present a stark assessment of human experience:

- **Dukkha:** Life inherently involves suffering and dissatisfaction.
- **Samudaya:** This suffering stems from craving and attachment.
- **Nirodha:** It's possible to end this suffering.
- **Magga:** There's a path to liberation from suffering.

These truths build on each other, starting with the recognition of life's inherent challenges and culminating in the possibility of transcendence. They suggest that by letting go of attachments and cultivating wisdom, we can find freedom from suffering.

The Eightfold Path offers a practical guide for this journey:

- **Right View:** Understanding reality's true nature
- **Right Intention:** Cultivating wholesome motivations

- **Right Speech:** Communicating truthfully and helpfully
- **Right Action:** Engaging in ethical conduct
- **Right Livelihood:** Earning a living without causing harm
- **Right Effort:** Cultivating positive mental states
- **Right Mindfulness:** Developing present-moment awareness
- **Right Concentration:** Cultivating focused attention

These aren't sequential steps but interconnected aspects of a holistic approach to personal growth. They work in concert, each reinforcing the others.

In the context of MBSR, certain elements of these teachings align closely with the program's goals. The recognition of suffering and the cultivation of mindfulness are central to MBSR's approach to stress reduction and well-being.

However, MBSR faces a challenge: how to integrate this wisdom without compromising its secular nature. Principles like Right Speech and Right Action, while valuable, risk introducing religious elements into a nonreligious program.

The task is to extract universal insights while setting aside culturally specific elements. How can we incorporate these teachings' practical benefits while maintaining an inclusive, nonreligious approach? Which aspects transcend cultural boundaries, and which are inextricably tied to a Buddhist worldview?

By grappling with these questions, you can gain insight into MBSR's careful balancing act. The goal isn't to replicate Buddhist practices, but to distill their wisdom into a form relevant and accessible in our diverse, modern world.

The Four Foundations of Mindfulness

You can regard the Four Foundations of Mindfulness as a roadmap for navigating the labyrinth of human experience. Detailed in the *Satipatthāna Sutta*,[3] a cornerstone of Theravada Buddhism, these foundations offer a systematic approach to cultivating awareness and insight:

- Mindfulness of the Body (*kaya*)
- Mindfulness of Feelings (*vedana*)
- Mindfulness of Mind States (*citta*)
- Mindfulness of Phenomena (*dhamma*)

These are interconnected pathways to deeper understanding. They work in concert, each amplifying the others, guiding practitioners toward a comprehensive grasp of their lived experience.

Mindfulness of the Body is about becoming intimately acquainted with your physical self. It's noticing the subtle rise and fall of your breath, the sensation of your feet against the Earth as you walk.

Mindfulness of Feelings focuses on recognizing the tones of experience, whether pleasant, unpleasant, or neutral. The goal? Observing without getting entangled, fostering equanimity in the face of life's ever-changing landscape.

Mindfulness of Mind States involves paying attention to the quality and content of your mental experiences. It's about observing thoughts and emotions arise and dissipate, without getting caught in their currents.

Mindfulness of Phenomena delves deeper, exploring Buddhist concepts like the Five Hindrances and the Seven Factors of Awakening. It's about applying Buddhist teachings to direct experience.

In MBSR, these foundations are reimagined for a secular context:

- The body scan and mindful movement embody Mindfulness of the Body, grounding participants in their physical experience.
- Observing the quality of experiences as pleasant, unpleasant, or neutral reflects Mindfulness of Feelings, fostering a balanced relationship with life's ups and downs.

- Noticing mental states during meditation mirrors Mindfulness of Mind States, enhancing self-awareness and emotional regulation.
- Mindfulness of Phenomena is less explicitly taught, a deliberate choice to maintain MBSR's secular nature.

This adaptation is both a strength and a limitation. It makes mindfulness more accessible to a diverse audience, but potentially misses opportunities for deeper exploration.

The Four Foundations of Mindfulness offer a comprehensive framework for cultivating awareness. In MBSR, they're adapted into secular practices that help participants develop self-awareness and emotional balance.

Ehipassiko: The Invitation to Investigate

The Buddha's invitation was simple yet revolutionary: "Come and see." This principle, *ehipassiko*, isn't about blind faith or mental gymnastics. It's a call to action, an empirical approach to understanding reality.

Imagine a scientist presenting a potentially groundbreaking theory. True scientists don't demand blind acceptance of their findings or theories; they invite verification. That's *ehipassiko* in action.

This emphasis on direct investigation is the beating heart of MBSR. There's a saying among MBSR teachers: "MBSR is caught, not taught." While instruction plays a role, the essence of the practice is experiential. Participants don't just learn about mindfulness; they live it, moment by moment.

This approach echoes the Buddha's advice to the Kalama people. He urged them to rely not on hearsay, tradition, or even his own words, but on their personal experiences. It's a classic example of critical thinking in spiritual practice.

This provides a practical method for gaining insight. Through meditation and mindfulness, practitioners turn their attention inward, observing their own body, feelings, mind, and mental objects. It's like becoming the scientist and the experiment simultaneously.

The goal? To gain firsthand insight into experiences like impermanence, suffering, and the nature of self. These aren't abstract concepts to memorize, but realities to be explored through direct observation.

> **Note:** MBSR embodies this spirit of investigation. It doesn't ask participants to dogmatically accept or assume; it invites them to explore. The benefits aren't theoretical; they're personal and tangible. This empirical approach has allowed MBSR to adapt Buddhist practices for secular contexts, making mindfulness more accessible without requiring adherence to any belief system.

Consider your own most profound learning experiences. They likely came not from passive acceptance, but from active investigation and firsthand experience.

The invitation to investigate reminds us that mindfulness isn't about accepting doctrines. It's about discovering our own truths. By maintaining this spirit of open inquiry, MBSR offers a transformative yet accessible path to greater well-being.

As we continue to refine MBSR and develop Open MBSR, *ehipassiko* serves as our North Star. It challenges us to keep the practice grounded in direct experience, to remain open to new discoveries, and to continually verify our methods' effectiveness.

The question for practitioners and teachers is this: How can they embody this spirit of investigation in their practice and teaching? How can they encourage others to "come and see" for themselves, rather than simply accepting what they're told about mindfulness?

By staying true to this principle, we ensure that mindfulness remains a living, breathing practice rather than a mindless set of dogmas to be blindly followed. We invite each person to become their own scientist, exploring amid the vast laboratory of their own experience.

Other Buddhist Concepts That Influence MBSR

The tendrils of Buddhist thought reach far beyond MBSR's curriculum, weaving their way into teacher training and informal discussions. This subtle yet pervasive influence shapes how MBSR is taught and understood, creating a complex tapestry of ancient wisdom and modern practice.

In conversations with MBSR teachers, certain Buddhist concepts consistently emerge as crucial elements in their training and approach. These ideas, while not explicitly part of the MBSR curriculum, form an invisible foundation that supports and informs the practice.

The Four Immeasurables

The Four Immeasurables, a cornerstone of Buddhist thought, have quietly infiltrated MBSR, shaping its approach far beyond the official curriculum. These ancient concepts, loving-kindness, compassion, appreciative joy, and equanimity, are whispered in teacher training and informal conversations, their influence subtle yet pervasive.

- **Loving-kindness:** A warm, expansive goodwill toward all beings.
- **Compassion:** The heart's response to suffering, coupled with the wish to alleviate it.
- **Appreciative joy:** The ability to delight in others' happiness and good fortune.
- **Equanimity:** Mental stability in the face of life's ups and downs.

The Four Immeasurables stand as pillars of Buddhist thought, their roots reaching deep into ancient scriptures like the *Pali Canon*. All of these qualities—loving-kindness, compassion, appreciative joy, and equanimity—are positioned as antidotes to the mind's afflictions:

greed, hatred, delusion, and fear. They are practical tools for navigating life's complexities.

- *Loving-kindness* radiates as a warm, expansive goodwill toward all beings. In MBSR, it might surface through *meta meditation,* where participants silently repeat well-wishes for themselves and others. It's a practice of cultivating universal friendliness, removed from of its religious context.
- *Compassion* emerges as the heart's response to suffering, coupled with a desire to alleviate it. While not explicitly taught in MBSR, it's woven into the fabric of the program, evident in the approach to difficulties with patience and nonjudgment.
- *Appreciative joy* celebrates others' happiness and good fortune, standing in opposition to envy. Though not directly addressed in MBSR, it might be evoked through shared poetry, highlighting life's inherent beauty and abundance.
- *Equanimity* stands as mental stability amid life's tumultuous nature. MBSR emphasizes this quality, aiming to develop participants' capacity to weather both pleasant and unpleasant experiences without being overwhelmed.

In Buddhist tradition, these qualities are viewed as essential for spiritual growth and enlightenment. They're tools for purifying the mind and generating positive Karma. The Buddha taught them as a means to cultivate a mind free from hostility and ill will.

Buddhist practitioners cultivate these qualities through specific meditation techniques, systematically generating these feelings toward themselves, loved ones, neutral persons, difficult people, and ultimately all beings. The goal? To make these qualities spontaneous and effortless, permeating every aspect of life.

The Three Characteristics

The Three Characteristics, or Three Marks of Existence, stand as pillars of Buddhist philosophy. First taught by the Buddha in the

Dhammacakkappavattana Sutta,[4] these foundational truths offer a lens through which to view all phenomena:

- Impermanence (*anicca*)
- Suffering (*dukkha*)
- Nonself (*anatta*)

These ancient concepts, while profound, present a unique challenge when integrated into a modern, secular program like MBSR.

- *Impermanence* speaks to the ever-changing nature of all phenomena. Like a river that never contains the same water twice, our experiences are in constant flux. Through mindfulness, we observe this ceaseless ebb and flow of sensations, thoughts, and emotions. In MBSR, impermanence is relatively straightforward to incorporate. It's observable and aligns with scientific understanding, allowing participants to notice the changing nature of their experiences without adopting any specific belief system.
- *Dukkha*, often translated as suffering, goes deeper. It points to the inherent lack of satisfaction when grasping at impermanent things. It's akin to clutching at water: The tighter we grip, the more it slips away. Recognizing impermanence can lead to a natural letting go, bringing relief from this suffering. In MBSR, the concept of suffering as a result of grasping is trickier to convey. Rather than presenting it as universal truth, teachers might frame it as an inquiry: "How does holding tightly to certain experiences contribute to your stress?"
- *Nonself* challenges our notion of a fixed identity. When we look closely, we find no unchanging core, only a series of ever-shifting processes. It's like peeling an onion only to find there's no center. This insight can uproot the deep attachment to self that often fuels our distress. Nonself is perhaps the most challenging concept to integrate into MBSR. It's often approached

indirectly by focusing on the fluid nature of thoughts and emotions, naturally leading to questions about the nature of self and the relationship between observer and observed.

These concepts intertwine with dependent origination: the idea that all phenomena arise and cease based on interconnected causes and conditions. In Buddhist practice, these insights are cultivated through *vipassana* meditation, aiming to liberate practitioners from ignorance and craving, ultimately leading to *Nibbana*, which is the complete cessation of suffering.

Integrating these concepts into MBSR requires careful adaptation. The goal is to translate these insights into practical tools that remain accessible and deeply insightful, without veering into metaphysical territory that might alienate participants. This delicate balance forms the crux of the exploration into disentangling mindfulness from its Buddhist roots while preserving its transformative power.

Yogic Influences

Yoga, an ancient Indian system of philosophy and practice deeply rooted in Hindu and Buddhist traditions, plays a crucial role in MBSR, distinguishing it from other mindfulness interventions. To understand its significance, we must first explore its rich spiritual heritage and key concepts.

Yoga, Sanskrit for "union," is a comprehensive system aimed at uniting the individual self with the divine or universal consciousness. Originating in the Vedic traditions of ancient India over 5,000 years ago, yoga encompasses various practices designed to achieve physical, mental, and spiritual well-being. These include:

- **Asanas (physical postures):** Originally designed to prepare the body for meditation, these postures have spiritual significance in aligning the physical body with cosmic energies.
- **Pranayama (breath regulation):** Rooted in the concept of prana (life force), these techniques are believed to control vital energy and purify the mind and body.

- **Dhyana (meditation):** A central practice in Hindu and Buddhist traditions, dhyana is aimed at achieving higher states of consciousness and spiritual insight.
- **Yamas and Niyamas (ethical principles):** These form the moral and behavioral guidelines in classical yoga philosophy, emphasizing virtues like nonviolence, truthfulness, and contentment.

Hatha yoga, a specific branch developed around the 11th century, emphasizes physical postures and breathing techniques. The term "hatha" combines "ha" (sun) and "tha" (moon), symbolizing the balance of opposite energies. While it forms the foundation for many modern Western yoga styles, its original purpose was to prepare practitioners for deeper spiritual practices and ultimate liberation.

In MBSR, Jon Kabat-Zinn integrates a specific approach he terms "mindful hatha yoga" or "mindfulness of yoga." This practice is a core component of the MBSR program, alongside the body scan and sitting meditation. Kabat-Zinn (2013) explains:

> Mindful hatha yoga is the third major formal meditation practice that we make use of in MBSR, along with the body scan and sitting meditation. It consists of gentle stretching, strengthening, and balancing exercises, done very slowly, with moment-to-moment awareness of breathing and of the sensations that arise as you put your body into various configurations known as "postures."

This approach emphasizes the mind–body connection, using physical sensations as anchors for present-moment awareness. The focus is not on achieving perfect form or increased flexibility, but on cultivating a deep awareness of the body and breath in each moment.

Kabat-Zinn further emphasizes the holistic nature of this practice: "Mindful yoga is also an extremely effective way in which you can learn about yourself and come to experience yourself as whole, regardless of your physical condition or level of fitness" (Kabat-Zinn, 2013).

The integration of mindful hatha yoga in MBSR serves several key purposes:

- **Embodied mindfulness:** It provides a tangible way to experience mindfulness through bodily sensations, making the abstract concept of mindfulness more concrete and accessible.
- **Accessibility:** The gentle nature of the practice makes it suitable for diverse populations, including those with physical limitations or no prior yoga experience.
- **Experiential learning:** It allows participants to explore fundamental mindfulness concepts through direct experience. For instance, holding a challenging pose can teach about impermanence and nonattachment.
- **Holistic approach:** MBSR recognizes the interconnectedness of body and mind, using yoga as a bridge between physical and mental aspects of well-being.

The mindful hatha yoga in MBSR differs from traditional hatha yoga classes in several ways:

- **Focus:** The primary goal is cultivating awareness, not physical fitness or mastering poses.
- **Intensity:** It's generally gentler and more accessible than typical yoga classes.
- **Integration:** It's seamlessly woven into the broader mindfulness curriculum, not treated as a separate practice.

This integration of mindful hatha yoga into MBSR creates a comprehensive approach to mindfulness, reminding practitioners that mindfulness isn't solely a mental exercise but a whole-body experience. As MBSR continues to evolve, this embodied approach to mindfulness remains crucial. It offers practitioners a direct, experiential way to cultivate present-moment awareness, fostering a deeper connection between body, breath, and mind.

The Nine Attitudes of Mindfulness

The Nine Attitudes of Mindfulness were defined by Jon Kabat-Zinn in *Full Catastrophe Living*, a book often recommended as supplementary reading in MBSR courses. In prominent MBSR teacher training programs, instructors learn to embody these attitudes rather than teach them explicitly, allowing them to emerge naturally through the practice. This approach reflects the understanding that mindfulness is best taught through example rather than direct instruction. While these attitudes have parallels in Buddhist thought that I explore later, it's important to note that these connections are interpretive rather than explicitly drawn by Kabat-Zinn.

Let's break down each attitude:

- **Nonjudging:** Letting go of goals and allowing yourself to simply be, which paradoxically leads to growth and change. This reflects both the Daoist concept of *wei-wu-wei* (action through nonaction) and the Buddhist concept of *santoṣa* (contentment). Wei-wu-wei teaches that effective action comes from aligning with the natural flow rather than forcing outcomes, while Buddhist teachings emphasize the futility of craving (taṇhā) as described in the Four Noble Truths.
- **Patience:** Allowing experiences to unfold naturally, recognizing that things emerge in their own time. This connects to khanti in Buddhism's 10 perfections and appears in the *Khantivadi Jataka*, which illustrates the power of patience through the tale of an ascetic who maintains tranquility even in the face of severe persecution.
- **Beginner's mind:** Approaching each moment with fresh eyes, free from preconceptions. This embodies the Zen concept of shoshin, extensively explored in both Chinese Chan and Japanese Zen traditions through koans and direct instruction.

- **Trust:** Developing confidence in one's inner wisdom and direct experience. This parallels the Buddhist concept of saddhā (faith) and the Mahayana teaching of Buddha-nature, suggesting everyone's innate capacity for awareness and wisdom.
- **Non-striving:** Observing experiences without categorizing them as good or bad. This attitude reflects both Buddhist equanimity (*upekkhā*) and the Daoist concept of wei-wu-wei, where we accomplish more by suspending our habitual reactions.
- **Acceptance:** Clear acknowledgment of the present moment without resistance. This mirrors the Buddhist concept of *tathatā* (suchness) and *yathābhūta-ñāṇadassana* (seeing things as they are).
- **Letting go:** Nonattachment to experiences, recognizing their impermanent nature. This directly relates to *nekkhamma* (renunciation) and *vairāgya* (dispassion) in Buddhist practice, with the Dhammapada specifically addressing letting go of past, present, and future.
- **Gratitude:** Appreciating life's countless supports and nourishments. While not explicitly named in early Buddhism, this connects to both *kataññutā* (gratitude) and *muditā* (appreciative joy), with the *Kataññu Sutta* specifically addressing its importance.
- **Generosity:** Cultivating an open, receptive state of mind and heart. This mirrors dāna, the first of Buddhism's 10 perfections, seen as foundational to spiritual development and discussed extensively in texts like the *Dāna Sutta*.

While rooted in Buddhist teachings, the Nine Attitudes of Mindfulness are presented in MBSR within a secular context, emphasizing their universal relevance. These attitudes are practical tools for navigating life's challenges, enriching the mindfulness process, and fostering a deeper sense of clarity, compassion, and balance. By integrating these foundational principles into the MBSR framework, the program ensures that the wisdom behind these attitudes remains accessible and impactful, contributing to the overall effectiveness and inclusivity of mindfulness practices in a modern, secular setting.

Bridging Ancient Wisdom and Modern Practice: The MBSR Synthesis

This chapter has journeyed deep into the heart of MBSR, unearthing its Buddhist and yogic roots. It traced how awareness of breath, body scan, open awareness, and loving-kindness were carefully adapted from their original contexts for contemporary practitioners.

It then explored the foundational Buddhist concepts underlying these practices—the Three Jewels, the Four Noble Truths, and the Eightfold Path—showing how they inform MBSR's approach. The Four Foundations of Mindfulness emerged as a key framework for developing awareness, while *ehipassiko* (come and see for yourself) highlighted MBSR's emphasis on direct experience.

The exploration of additional Buddhist concepts like the Four Immeasurables and the Three Characteristics revealed their subtle influence on mindfulness teaching. The integration of mindful yoga demonstrated MBSR's holistic approach to embodied practice, while the Nine Attitudes of Mindfulness showed how Buddhist wisdom can be effectively translated for modern contexts.

Throughout, you've encountered the essential question of progression: How can mindfulness programs effectively adapt to modern needs while honoring the rich wisdom from contemplative traditions?

Key Takeaways

- Buddhist contemplative practices and concepts form the foundation of MBSR's core practices, although they have been adapted for secular contexts.

- The Four Foundations of Mindfulness provide a systematic framework for developing awareness that shapes how MBSR approaches mindfulness practice.

- The principle of *ehipassiko* (come and see for yourself) fundamentally guides MBSR's emphasis on direct experience and personal investigation.
- MBSR's integration of mindful yoga creates an embodied approach to mindfulness that bridges ancient yogic wisdom with contemporary practice.
- The Nine Attitudes of Mindfulness demonstrate how Buddhist concepts can be effectively translated into accessible tools for modern practitioners.
- MBSR's evolution from Buddhist roots shows both the possibilities and challenges of adapting contemplative practices for contemporary needs.

Reflection Questions

1. How can understanding the origins and adaptations of MBSR's practices inform future innovations in mindfulness teaching?
2. What role should transparency about Buddhist roots play in secular mindfulness programs?
3. How might mindfulness programs evolve while maintaining the essence of contemplative practice?

Looking Ahead

Having traced MBSR's Buddhist roots, we stand at a pivotal juncture in mindfulness teaching. While these contemplative traditions offer profound wisdom, they need not constrain future development. Chapter 4 explores how diverse influences, from contemplative science to open-source principles, can inform the progression of mindfulness programs. These perspectives offer fresh approaches for making mindfulness more accessible and adaptable while learning from its contemplative heritage.

Chapter 4

Inspirations from Unlikely Sources

This chapter transitions from exploring MBSR's foundations to envisioning its future. The past has laid a rich groundwork, but the future demands innovation. This chapter serves as a bridge, connecting what has been with what could be.

The journey into Open MBSR draws inspiration from unexpected places. Like a curious traveler stumbling upon hidden gems, we've gathered insights from diverse fields that, at first glance, might seem unrelated to mindfulness. Yet it's often at these intersections of disparate ideas that true innovation flourishes.

This chapter explores the following wellsprings of inspiration:

- Contemplative science
- Acceptance and Commitment Therapy (ACT)
- The Agile methodology
- Open source
- Quakerism
- Humanism

Each offers a unique perspective, sometimes overlapping, sometimes contrasting, but always illuminating. They challenge you to think beyond the confines of the current norms and traditions and envision a more adaptable, inclusive approach.

This approach does not discard the wisdom of the past. Rather, it builds on that foundation, infusing it with fresh insights to create something both timeless and timely. It's not merely tweaking MBSR; it's reimagining its potential to serve humanity in our rapidly evolving world.

As I delve into these influences, I am not just gathering information. I am embarking on a transformative journey, one that will reshape the understanding of mindfulness and its role in fostering human flourishing. This exploration is an act of creation, weaving together diverse threads to form a new tapestry of understanding.

The goal is ambitious: to synthesize these insights into a comprehensive framework that honors the complexity of human experience. Open MBSR aims to empower individuals to cultivate resilience, deepen connections, and nurture well-being amid life's constant changes.

This chapter serves as a model of transparency, pulling back the curtain on the thought processes and influences shaping Open MBSR. It's an invitation to engage critically and creatively with these ideas, to question assumptions, and to envision new possibilities.

I urge you to embark on this exploration with the curiosity of a child and the discernment of a sage. Each influence offers a piece of the puzzle, but it's up to you to fit them together in meaningful ways. This journey into these diverse fields isn't just about expanding our knowledge; it's about expanding our perspective and sparking innovation.

The path ahead is uncharted, filled with potential and challenges alike. But it's in navigating this unknown territory that you have the opportunity to create something truly revolutionary. Step forward with an open mind and curious heart, ready to discover new pathways to a more inclusive, effective, and transformative approach to mindfulness.

Contemplative Science: Unity and Depth Without Dogma

Contemplative science stands at the crossroads of ancient wisdom and modern inquiry. It's a field born from the collision of timeless contemplative practices and the rigorous methodology of scientific research. This convergence didn't happen by chance. It was catalyzed by the rise of MBSR, which offered a secular framework for mindfulness that resonated with Western audiences and piqued the interest of researchers.

The Mind and Life Institute, a brainchild of neuroscientist Francisco Varela, entrepreneur Adam Engle, and the Dalai Lama, became a crucible for this emerging field. It fostered dialogues between Western scientists and Buddhist practitioners, exploring how meditation could be studied and validated through scientific methods. This collaboration shaped the trajectory of contemplative science, weaving together Eastern practices and Western empiricism.

One of contemplative science's most potent strengths lies in its ability to unify diverse intentions within a shared practice. Whether approached from a spiritual, therapeutic, or performance-oriented perspective, mindfulness and meditation offer universal benefits.

This approach allows for depth without dogma. It maintains the substance of mindfulness practices without tethering them to specific religious or spiritual frameworks. The rich body of research around consciousness contemplation stands independent of any particular belief system. For some, mindfulness carries spiritual significance; for others, it's interpreted through a secular, philosophical, or scientific lens. Contemplative science respects these differences while unifying practitioners under the shared goal of exploring the human mind and improving well-being.

However, this field isn't without its critics. Philosopher Evan Thompson (2020) warns of "neural Buddhism," wherein Buddhist practices are validated through neuroscience, potentially compromising scientific objectivity. Miguel Farias and Catherine Wikholm (2015) echo these concerns in *The Buddha Pill: Can Meditation Change You?* highlighting the risk of confirmation bias in research closely tied to Buddhist figures.

These critiques serve as crucial reminders. While contemplative science offers valuable insights, maintaining scientific rigor and objectivity is paramount. The field has responded with improved methodological rigor, emphasizing double-blind studies, diverse research teams, and peer review.

The integration of contemplative science into MBSR has been symbiotic from the start. It has bolstered MBSR's credibility in clinical settings and beyond, providing empirical support for its efficacy. This scientific underpinning creates an inclusive environment, bridging the gap between skeptics and seasoned practitioners.

Yet the influence of Buddhist concepts on research agendas presents a challenge. The Buddhist entanglement raises important questions about objectivity in research and the secular nature of MBSR. These issues demand careful consideration and will be further explored in the next chapter.

The path ahead requires a delicate balance. We must honor traditional practices while incorporating new scientific insights. This ongoing dialogue between contemplative traditions and scientific research will shape the future of MBSR, solidifying its position at the forefront of mindfulness-based interventions in our ever-evolving world.

Contemplative science offers a wealth of insights that can shape the future of Open MBSR. This field's contributions illuminate three key pathways for evolution, described next.

Inclusivity Through Scientific Framing

Open MBSR, armed with the robust findings of contemplative science, speaks a language that resonates with skeptics and believers alike. It's not about chanting in dimly lit rooms or achieving enlightenment overnight. Instead, it's about tangible, measurable benefits that touch every aspect of our lives. This scientific approach doesn't strip mindfulness of its depth; rather, it illuminates its universal applicability, making it as relevant in the boardroom as it is in the meditation hall.

Personal Interpretation

Contemplative science informs Open MBSR's recognition of the diverse landscape of human motivation. It offers a framework adaptable to various intentions, whether cognitive training, psychological intervention, or spiritual exploration. This approach doesn't prescribe a single path but empowers practitioners to chart their own course. A neuroscientist might approach mindfulness as a fascinating cognitive training ground, a spiritual seeker views it as a gateway to deeper truths, while a trauma survivor might see it as a path to psychological healing. By accommodating this spectrum of goals, Open MBSR creates a space where diverse interpretations enrich the collective experience, guided by scientific insight, yet open to personal meaning.

Common Language

Contemplative science offers Open MBSR a bridge, a common vocabulary that transcends individual backgrounds and beliefs. This shared language isn't about creating an exclusive club. Instead, it's a tool for clarity, allowing participants to articulate their experiences with precision and depth. It connects personal insights to broader scientific discourse, elevating everyday practice to a part of a larger, ongoing dialogue about the nature of mind and well-being.

These elements go well beyond simply teaching mindfulness; they cultivate a community of mindful explorers, each charting their own course but united by a common quest for understanding and growth. This is mindfulness for the modern age: scientifically grounded, personally relevant, and universally accessible.

Acceptance and Commitment Therapy (ACT)

In the landscape of mental health, a radical approach emerged in the 1980s. Psychologist Steven C. Hayes developed Acceptance and Commitment Therapy (ACT), challenging our relationship with difficult thoughts and emotions. ACT's core mission? To cultivate psychological flexibility: our ability to stay present and act on our values, even when our minds scream otherwise.

Embracing Paradox

The heart of ACT lies in its audacious embrace of contradiction. It's right there in the name: Acceptance and Commitment Therapy. At first glance, these concepts seem to be locked in an eternal tug-of-war. How can we accept our circumstances while simultaneously committing to change them? It's a tension that most of us spend our lives trying to resolve, often fruitlessly.

But ACT doesn't seek to eliminate this tension. Instead, it invites us to dance with it, to find the hidden harmony within the discord. This is where the true power of the approach reveals itself. We are not bound to choose between acceptance and action; instead, we may effectively learn to wield both simultaneously.

Think of it like holding two ends of a rubber band. Pull too hard on either side and it snaps. But find the right balance, and you create a dynamic tension that can propel you forward with surprising force.

This paradoxical approach offers a more nuanced view of personal growth. It suggests that real change doesn't come from constantly battling against our experiences or trying to strong-arm our way through life. Instead, it emerges when we fully embrace our reality, the good, the bad, and the ugly, while simultaneously taking purposeful steps toward what truly matters to us.

It's a challenging concept to grasp, precisely because our minds crave simplicity and clear-cut solutions. But life rarely offers us such neat packages. By learning to hold these seemingly opposing forces in balance, we develop a kind of psychological agility that allows us to navigate the messiness of existence with far greater skill and grace.

This approach doesn't just apply to our internal struggles. It's a lens through which we can view the world at large, helping us to transcend the false dichotomies that often trap us in rigid thinking and limited perspectives. We strive to expand our capacity to see the full spectrum of human experience, rather than getting stuck in black-and-white judgments.

The ACT Hexaflex: A Model for Psychological Flexibility

ACT is often represented visually as a hexagon, known as the *ACT Hexaflex*. This model outlines six core processes that work together to build psychological flexibility:

- **Acceptance:** Embracing our experiences without trying to change them

- **Cognitive defusion:** Creating distance from our thoughts, rather than being entangled in them
- **Being present:** Engaging fully with the here and now
- **Self as context:** Observing our experiences from a place of curious awareness
- **Values:** Identifying what truly matters to us
- **Committed action:** Taking steps aligned with our values

These processes aren't isolated skills. They're interconnected facets of a more flexible, adaptive way of engaging with life.

Integrating ACT in MBSR

ACT offers a unique perspective that can enrich our understanding of Open MBSR:

- **The paradox principle:** ACT's core tenet—accepting what we can't change while committing to action where possible—mirrors the complexity Open MBSR addresses. It reminds us that growth often lies in the tension between opposing forces.
- **Values as compass:** While Open MBSR cultivates present-moment awareness, ACT's emphasis on values can provide a deeper "why" to our practice. It's about being present with purpose.
- **From insight to action:** ACT's focus on committed action might offer a bridge between meditation insights and real-world application. It asks, "How can we translate this awareness into meaningful change?"
- **The observing self:** ACT's concept of "self as context" aligns with and potentially deepens MBSR's approach to meta-awareness. It's about cultivating a stable vantage point from which to witness our ever-changing experience.

- **Defusing from thoughts:** Both approaches encourage a different relationship with our mental content. ACT's cognitive defusion techniques can complement MBSR's nonjudgmental awareness, offering additional tools for psychological flexibility.

This exploration is designed to open a dialogue, to see where these approaches might inform and enrich each other. By considering ACT's principles, one might uncover new dimensions in Open MBSR; not as a dramatic shift, but as a natural evolution of its core mission. It's an invitation to look at familiar terrain through a slightly different lens, potentially revealing new paths and possibilities not yet considered.

The Agile Revolution

In the annals of innovation, few methodologies have left as indelible a mark as Agile. Born from the crucible of the 1990s software crisis, Agile emerged as a beacon of hope in a sea of rigid, outdated practices. It's a story of adaptation, of individuals daring to challenge the status quo, and of a movement that grew from the ground up.

Picture this: It's the late 1990s, and software projects are sinking faster than the *Titanic*, weighed down by bureaucracy and inflexibility. The dominant approach, Waterfall, demands extensive upfront planning, rigid sequential phases, and little room for adjustment. By the time teams deliver a product, market conditions, customer needs, and even the technology itself have often changed. The industry is crying out for a lifeline.

Enter Agile, not as a savior descending from on high, but as a collective realization among those in the trenches. Unlike Waterfall, Agile embraces change as a constant. It prioritizes adaptability over prediction, collaboration over silos, and working software over exhaustive documentation.

The Agile Manifesto, penned in 2001 by 17 forward-thinking developers, wasn't just a document; it was a declaration of independence from the tyranny of rigid methodologies. Its four core values read like a revolutionary's creed:

- Individuals and interactions over processes and tools
- Working software over comprehensive documentation
- Customer collaboration over contract negotiation
- Responding to change over following a plan

These weren't just lofty ideals. They were battle-tested principles, forged in the fires of real-world projects and tempered by the wisdom of experience.

Agile's true power lay not in its principles alone, but in how it spread. This wasn't a top-down mandate or a consultant's PowerPoint presentation. Agile grew like a wildfire, ignited by the passion of practitioners who had experienced its benefits firsthand and couldn't keep quiet about it. It was a grassroots revolution, driven by small teams proving that working software could be delivered faster, better, and with less waste.

Instead of long, rigid development cycles, Agile introduced Minimum Viable Products (MVPs): early, functional versions designed for real-world feedback. Teams embraced iterative development, continuously refining and improving rather than betting everything on a single, large-scale release. Constant communication, through daily stand-ups and sprint reviews, ensured alignment and adaptability. And with regular updates based on actual outcomes, Agile teams stayed responsive, making course corrections in real time rather than months too late.

This was a fundamental change in how work got done. Agile adapted and evolved as it touched new industries and contexts, proving itself far beyond the realm of software.

Now, as we stand at the crossroads of mindfulness practice, Open MBSR finds itself facing challenges eerily similar to those that spawned Agile. Traditional approaches often feel rigid, slow to adapt, and disconnected from the diverse needs of the practitioners.

Inspirations from Unlikely Sources

What if we applied the Agile mindset to mindfulness? Imagine an MBSR program that prioritizes individual experiences over rigid curricula, one that values practical results over theoretical purity, a program that collaborates deeply with its community and adapts swiftly to new insights and needs.

This isn't about abandoning the core of MBSR. It's about infusing it with the agility to thrive in our rapidly changing world. It's about creating a practice that's as dynamic and diverse as the minds it serves.

The Agile revolution shows us that transformation doesn't have to come from the top-down. It can start with us, the practitioners, the teachers, and the students. We have the power to evolve MBSR, to make it more responsive, more inclusive, and ultimately more impactful.

Agile + Mindfulness: Revolutionizing Open MBSR

The principles that transformed software development ultimately became a blueprint for evolution. And now they're knocking on the door of Open MBSR, offering a path to a more dynamic, responsive, and impactful practice. The following sections break down how these Agile ideas can reshape the approach to mindfulness.

Flexibility with a Backbone

Imagine an Open MBSR that bends without breaking. I'm talking about a framework that's clear enough to maintain integrity, yet flexible enough to adapt to diverse needs. It's not about throwing out the rulebook; it's about writing one that encourages innovation while preserving the essence of the practice.

The Art of Constant Becoming

In the Agile world, nothing is ever "finished." Apply this to Open MBSR, and you get a practice that's always evolving, always improving. Regular cycles of teaching, feedback, and refinement keep the program sharp and relevant, responsive to the latest research and the changing needs of practitioners.

Power to the People

The strength of Open MBSR lies not in a single "visionary" guru, but in the collective wisdom of its community. By fostering a collaborative ecosystem of teachers, practitioners, and researchers, we can tap into a wellspring of innovation and insight. It's mindfulness democracy in action.

Eyes on the Prize

Shift the focus from "how we've always done it" to "what we're trying to achieve." This outcome-focused approach allows Open MBSR to flex and adapt across different contexts while staying true to its core goals. The priority is effectiveness, not rigid adherence to a predefined method.

Radical Transparency

In a world drowning in misinformation, clarity is king. Open, honest communication about Open MBSR's practices, origins, and intentions builds trust and understanding. This isn't only fundamentally ethical; it's essential for building a thriving community.

The Goldilocks Zone

Finding the sweet spot between structure and innovation is an art. Too rigid, and we stifle creativity. Too loose, and we lose consistency. The goal is to create a framework that's "just right," providing enough guidance to ensure quality while leaving room for adaptation and growth.

Grassroots Growth

Empower Open MBSR graduates to form their own practice communities. These self-organizing groups extend the program's reach, creating a ripple effect of ongoing engagement and support. It's how a program becomes a movement.

By no means are we discarding the wisdom of traditional MBSR. Instead, we are infusing it with the agility to thrive in our rapidly changing world. By embracing these Agile principles, Open MBSR can become more than just a mindfulness program; it can be a living, breathing practice that grows and evolves with its community.

The Open Source Revolution: Unlocking the Power of Shared Knowledge

Throughout technological history, few movements have been as transformative, or as misunderstood, as open source. It's a tale of rebellion, of idealism colliding with pragmatism, and of a radical idea that reshaped the digital world.

Picture this: It's the 1970s. The fledgling software industry is locking down code, turning what was once freely shared into closely guarded secrets. But in the shadows, a resistance is brewing.

Enter Richard Stallman, a modern-day Robin Hood of the coding world. In 1983, he launches the GNU Project.[1] GNU stands for *Gnu's Not UNIX*, and Stallman's effort represents a bold attempt to create a completely free operating system. More than another software program, the GNU Project is a philosophical stand against the privatization of knowledge.

Stallman's GNU Manifesto reads like a declaration of independence for the digital age, articulating the philosophy of free software. This movement emphasized four essential freedoms:

- The freedom to run the program for any purpose
- The freedom to study and modify the program
- The freedom to redistribute copies
- The freedom to distribute modified versions

These aren't just technical specifications. They're a clarion call for a new way of thinking about creation and ownership in the information age.

Fast forward to 1998. A group of visionaries, including Eric Raymond and Bruce Perens, coin the term "open source." It's a strategic move, a rebranding of free software to make it palatable to the buttoned-up business world. But it's also the spark that ignites a revolution.

The impact? Nothing short of seismic. Today, open source is the invisible foundation of the digital world. It powers the servers that host websites, smartphones, and AI. It's not just a way of writing code, it's a philosophy that's reshaped how we think about collaboration, innovation, and the very nature of value creation.

The numbers tell a story of unstoppable growth. In 2022, 77 percent of organizations increased their use of open-source software. Its economic impact? A staggering $143 billion to $399 billion annually. That's a wholesale transformation of the technological landscape.

But open source is more than just lines of code or economic statistics. It's a testament to what humans can achieve when they tear down walls and work together. It's proof that transparency breeds trust, that collaboration trumps competition, and that the best ideas can come from anywhere.

As we stand on the cusp of a new era in mindfulness practice, the lessons of open source beckon. What could MBSR become if we applied these principles of radical openness and collaboration? How might we unlock the collective wisdom of practitioners, teachers, and researchers worldwide?

The open-source movement shows us that when we share knowledge freely, we all grow richer. It enables the creation of a world where information flows freely, where innovation is a collective endeavor, and where the fruits of our labor benefit all of humanity.

The question isn't whether Open MBSR can learn from open source. The question is: Are we ready to embrace the transformative power of openness?

Unleashing the Power of Open Mindfulness

The open-source revolution didn't just change how people write code, it's changing how people think about knowledge itself.

And now it's time for MBSR to join the party. The following sections explain how the principles of open source can transform mindfulness practice.

Radical Transparency

Imagine an MBSR curriculum as open as the Linux kernel. Every technique, every teaching material laid bare for all to see. This isn't merely about sharing, it's about inviting the world to make it better. When we open our practices to scrutiny, we're not exposing weaknesses—we're inviting strength.

The Wisdom of Crowds

In the open-source world, the next game-changing idea could come from anyone, anywhere. Apply this to MBSR, and you've got a global brain trust of practitioners, teachers, and researchers all working to push the practice forward. This is more than collaboration; it's supercharged evolution.

Building Blocks of Mindfulness

Think of MBSR as a set of Lego blocks, not a monolith. Each component should be able to stand alone or snap together with others. This modularity isn't just about flexibility; it's about creating a practice that can adapt to any context, any need.

The Power to Fork

In open source, if the main project doesn't meet your needs, you *fork* it, creating your own version. Imagine specialized MBSR programs sprouting up for athletes, artists, or astronauts. It's not dilution, it's diversification, each new branch enriching the whole.

Democracy of Practice

Governance in open source isn't top-down, it's community-driven. Bringing this to MBSR means decisions about the practice's future are made not by a select few, but by the collective wisdom of its practitioners. This approach unlocks the true potential of a global community.

Freedom to Grow

Open licensing isn't just legal jargon, it's a philosophical stance. It says, "This knowledge belongs to everyone." By adopting open licensing for MBSR materials, we're not giving anything away; we're ensuring the practice can spread, adapt, and thrive in ways we can't even imagine yet.

This isn't about tearing down MBSR; it's about setting it free. It's about recognizing that the wisdom of mindfulness, like the power of open source, grows stronger when it's shared freely. The open-source movement shows that when we break down walls, when we collaborate without borders, we can create things of astonishing power and beauty. Now it's MBSR's turn to embrace this revolution. The question isn't whether MBSR can go open source. The question is: What untapped potential will be unleashed when it does?

The Silent Revolution: Quakerism's Radical Vision

In the tumultuous landscape of 17th-century England, a quiet revolution was brewing. While others shouted from pulpits and fought wars over doctrine, George Fox and his followers were sitting in silence, listening for the still, small voice within.

Quakerism emerged as a defiant cry against the spiritual hierarchies of the day. In an era when kings claimed divine right and priests held the keys to heaven, Fox dared to proclaim that every person, regardless of title, education, or social standing, had direct access to truth and wisdom. It was spiritual democracy in its purest form.

Quakerism's principles, discussed next, offer a provocative blueprint for reimagining Open MBSR.

The Power of Silence

Imagine a mindfulness practice where silence isn't just a tool, but the teacher itself. Quaker meetings often unfold in profound quiet, broken only when someone feels genuinely moved to speak. This creates space for authentic insight to emerge. What if Open MBSR embraced this radical trust in silence and in each practitioner's inner wisdom?

Equality as Spiritual Practice

In a Quaker meeting, there's no guru at the front of the room, no hierarchy of enlightenment. Everyone sits in a circle, symbolizing their spiritual equality, and based on the fundamental belief that wisdom can come from anyone, at any time. How might Open MBSR evolve if we truly embraced the idea that every practitioner, from novice to veteran, has valuable insights to offer?

Consensus: The Art of Collective Wisdom

Quakers don't vote; they seek unity. This doesn't mean everyone agrees, but that the group collectively discerns the best way forward. It's slow, sometimes frustrating, but profoundly respectful of every voice. What if Open MBSR adopted this model for evolution, seeking not just majority approval but deep, collective understanding?

Simplicity: The Core of What Matters

In a world of constant distraction and complexity, Quakers emphasize simplicity, in worship, in lifestyle, in focus. It's about stripping away the nonessential to reveal what truly matters. How might this principle reshape Open MBSR, helping us focus on the core elements that drive transformation?

Direct Experience: The Ultimate Teacher

Quakerism insists that each person can access divine wisdom directly, without intermediaries. This radical trust in individual experience challenges us to rethink the role of teachers in Open MBSR. What if we saw instructors not as gurus dispensing wisdom, but as facilitators helping each person access their own inner knowing?

Quakerism's influence extends far beyond religion. Its principles have shaped democracies, inspired social movements, and influenced business practices. Now, it offers a provocative model for evolving Open MBSR. What might Open MBSR become if we dared to embrace these principles?

Quaker Wisdom: A Blueprint for Open MBSR

The Quakers turned the entire concept of spiritual hierarchy on its head. Now, their radical vision offers a provocative roadmap for revolutionizing Open MBSR.

Dethroning the Guru

Imagine a mindfulness practice where there are no enlightened masters, no special transmissions of wisdom. Just people, sitting together, each as capable of profound insight as the next. It's about recognizing that true wisdom doesn't flow from top to bottom, but emerges from within each of us.

The Ultimate Teacher: Your Own Mind

In Quaker meetings, silence isn't empty; it's pregnant with possibility. What if Open MBSR embraced this radical trust in direct experience? Picture practice sessions where participants aren't just following guided meditations, but are exploring the vast landscape of their own consciousness. Each person is empowered to become their own guide.

The Circle of Equals

In a world obsessed with status and credentials, what if we created a space where everyone's voice carried equal weight? From the nervous newcomer to the seasoned practitioner, each perspective adds a vital piece to the puzzle. The goal is to tap into the collective wisdom that emerges when we truly listen to each other.

Power to the People

Imagine an Open MBSR where the curriculum isn't handed down from on high, but emerges organically from the community itself. Where each practice, each teaching is a living document, constantly refined by the collective experience of its practitioners.

The Art of Spiritual Minimalism

In a world of endless distractions and quick-fix solutions, the Quaker emphasis on simplicity feels revolutionary. What if Open MBSR stripped away the nonessentials, focusing laser-like on the core practices that drive transformation? The goal is to cut through the noise to reach what really matters.

I do not mean to suggest turning Open MBSR into a Quaker meeting. The lesson lies in recognizing that centuries ago, a group of radicals cracked the code on creating a spiritual practice that was profoundly egalitarian, deeply respectful of individual experience, and committed to collective wisdom.

By embracing these principles, Open MBSR has the potential to transcend the limitations of traditional teacher–student models. It can become a truly collaborative exploration of human consciousness, accessible to all, regardless of background or belief.

The question isn't whether we can apply Quaker principles to mindfulness. The question is: What untapped potential might we unleash if we do? Are we ready to create a practice that's not just open in name, but open in its very DNA?

This is about fundamentally reimagining what mindfulness practice can be in the 21st century. It's about creating a space where each person's inner wisdom is honored, where collective insight trumps individual authority, and where the practice itself evolves with the needs and experiences of its community.

The Rise of Reason: Secular Humanism

In the grand tapestry of human thought, secular humanism stands as a bold declaration: We, as humans, are capable of creating meaning, morality, and purpose without appealing to the supernatural. It's a philosophy born from the crucible of the Enlightenment, tempered by scientific revolution, and honed by centuries of philosophical debate.

The roots of secular humanism run deep, tracing back to ancient Greek philosophers who dared to question the gods. But its modern incarnation emerged in the aftermath of two world wars, when humanity grappled with unprecedented moral challenges and the limitations of traditional belief systems.

Picture the intellectual landscape of the early 20th century. Darwin's theory of evolution had shaken the foundations of religious cosmology. Einstein's relativity had rewritten the laws of physics. Freud's psychoanalysis had peered into the depths of the human psyche. In this ferment of ideas, a new way of thinking about human nature and our place in the universe was taking shape.

In 1933, a group of freethinkers, including John Dewey and Albert Einstein, signed the first *Humanist Manifesto*. This was a clarion call for a new approach to ethics, meaning, and human flourishing based on reason and evidence rather than revelation or tradition. Secular humanism would go on to have real-world impact:

- In education, humanist principles drove the push for universal, secular schooling that teaches critical thinking and scientific literacy.
- In politics, it fueled movements for separation of church and state, ensuring that governance is based on reason and collective welfare rather than religious doctrine.
- In ethics, it sparked new approaches to moral philosophy that don't rely on divine command but on human reason and empathy.
- In science, it championed unfettered inquiry and the rigorous application of the scientific method to all aspects of life.

The journey wasn't always smooth. Secular humanists faced (and still face) opposition from those who see their philosophy as a threat to traditional values or religious beliefs. But they persevered, driven by the conviction that humanity is capable of tremendous good without the need for supernatural guidance.

Key figures like Paul Kurtz, who founded the Center for Inquiry, and Carl Sagan, who brought the wonders of science to the masses, became the modern torchbearers of this movement. They showed that a life based on reason and evidence could be not only ethical, but also filled abundantly with awe, wonder, and profound meaning.

Today, secular humanism thrives as a dynamic, evolving worldview embraced by millions. The *Secular Humanist Manifesto III* explicitly acknowledges this evolutionary process, emphasizing that human knowledge, ethics, and values are not static but must adapt to new discoveries and societal shifts. This flexibility has allowed secular humanism to shape critical discussions on bioethics, environmental policy, and now, the rapid advancements in artificial intelligence. As AI reshapes industries, decision-making, and even our understanding of consciousness, secular humanism provides a framework for ensuring that these technologies serve human well-being rather than replace human agency.

As we stand on the cusp of a new era in mindfulness practice, secular humanism offers a provocative model for how we might approach spirituality and personal growth in a world increasingly shaped by scientific understanding and AI. It challenges us to create practices that are inclusive, evidence-based, and deeply committed to human flourishing, not because a higher power demands it, but because we, as humans, choose it.

Mindfulness for the Modern Age: Secular Humanism's Blueprint for Open MBSR

In the grand experiment of human progress, secular humanism stands as a testament to our capacity for reason, ethics, and meaning without supernatural crutches. It also offers a provocative roadmap for revolutionizing Open MBSR.

The Science of Inner Peace

Imagine a mindfulness practice built not on ancient scriptures, but on the bedrock of scientific inquiry. Every technique, every teaching is scrutinized under the microscope of empirical research. It's not about discarding wisdom, it's about verifying it, refining it, and pushing it to new frontiers.

Ethics Without Gods

In a world torn by moral relativism and religious dogma, what if we crafted an ethical framework for mindfulness rooted in reason and human values? Not commandments handed down from on high, but principles we choose because they demonstrably improve human flourishing. It's about creating guidelines that resonate whether you're a believer, an atheist, or anywhere in between.

Here and Now: The Ultimate Frontier

Forget transcendence; what if we framed mindfulness as the ultimate tool for navigating the messy, beautiful reality of human existence? It's not about escaping this world, but about diving deeper into it. Imagine curriculum that tackles real-world issues: How can mindfulness improve our relationships? Our work? Our societies? It's mindfulness not as spiritual bypass, but as a catalyst for engaged living.

The Inquiring Mind

Picture a mindfulness practice that doesn't just tolerate questions, but thrives on them. Where skepticism isn't a barrier to entry, but a valued part of the journey. What if every Open MBSR course included spirited debates about the effects and implications of these practices? It's not about undermining the practice; it's about strengthening it through rigorous inquiry.

The Power of Human Agency

Forget surrendering to a higher power; what if mindfulness was about claiming our power as conscious, capable human beings? Imagine framing these practices not as a path to enlightenment, but as tools for enhancing our ability to shape our lives and our world. It's mindfulness not as passive acceptance, but as a springboard for purposeful action.

Speaking Human

Language matters. What if we moved beyond the recontextualization of Buddhist terminology and spoke about mindfulness in clear, accessible terms that resonate whether you're a scientist, a skeptic, or a seeker? Imagine a style guide for Open MBSR that ensures every word we use invites rather than alienates. It's not about dumbing down; it's about opening up.

> **Note:** This isn't about stripping mindfulness of its depth or power. It's about grounding it in the best of human knowledge and values. It's about creating a practice that's as rigorous as it is inclusive, as ethical as it is effective.

By embracing these principles, Open MBSR has the potential to pioneer a truly modern approach to mindfulness, one that's evidence-based, ethically grounded, and open to all. It's about creating a practice that's as relevant in the laboratory as it is in the meditation hall.

The question isn't whether mindfulness can be secular and humanistic. The question is: What new frontiers of human potential might we unlock if we fully embrace this approach? Are we ready to create a mindfulness practice that's as revolutionary in the 21st century as the scientific method was in the 17th?

This is more than just tweaking a curriculum. It's about fundamentally reimagining what mindfulness can be in a world shaped by reason, science, and human values. It's about creating a practice that harnesses the modern world's full potential to foster human flourishing.

The secular humanists dared to imagine ethics without gods, meaning without myth. Now it's our turn. Are we ready to create a mindfulness practice that's as bold, as rational, and as deeply human?

The Alchemy of Innovation

We stand at a crossroads in the evolution of mindfulness practice. The path forward isn't about choosing between tradition and innovation, but about forging a new way that honors both. This is the essence of Open MBSR: a bold reimagining of what mindfulness can be in our rapidly changing world.

Key Takeaways

- Contemplative science offers us a compass, guiding us toward practices that are both deeply transformative and scientifically sound.

- ACT grounds our awareness in values and action, ensuring our practice goes beyond feeling good to truly living well.

- Agile methodology provides a blueprint for evolution, allowing our practices to grow and adapt with the needs of our community.

- Open source principles unlock the collective genius of practitioners worldwide, democratizing access to wisdom that was once guarded.

- Quaker insights challenge us to dismantle hierarchies and trust in the profound wisdom that emerges from shared silence.

- Secular humanism reminds us that meaning and ethics don't require supernatural beliefs: They're rooted in our shared humanity.

The goal is to build on the wisdom of the past, infusing it with fresh insights to create something both timeless and timely. This is not merely tweaking MBSR; it's reimagining its potential to serve humanity in our rapidly evolving world.

Reflection Questions

1. How might this integrated approach reshape not just individual practice, but entire institutions dedicated to mindfulness and well-being?
2. What new frontiers of human flourishing could we unlock by embracing these diverse influences?
3. How can we ensure that, as Open MBSR evolves, it remains true to its core mission of alleviating suffering and fostering greater awareness?

Looking Ahead

The future of mindfulness isn't set in stone: It's clay in our hands, waiting to be shaped. Open MBSR offers us the tools, the vision, and the community to mold that future. The only question that remains is: Are we bold enough to seize this opportunity?

This is our chance to create a practice that's as dynamic and diverse as the minds it serves. A practice that's rigorous yet accessible, grounded in science yet open to mystery. A practice that doesn't just change individuals, but has the potential to transform our world.

The revolution in mindfulness isn't coming; it's already here. And with Open MBSR, we're not just witnessing it; we're creating it, together.

Part II

The Three Fundamental Problems

The mindfulness movement is sleepwalking toward irrelevance. While millions experience life-changing benefits, the very structures meant to share these practices are slowly poisoning them from within. Like a house built on eroding ground, the damage isn't immediately visible—but the foundation is crumbling.

What follows will likely unsettle you. It should. If you've invested years in mindfulness practice, if you teach or lead programs, if you've built your identity around certain approaches—prepare to be challenged. This isn't gentle meditation guidance. This is a wake-up call, and sometimes waking up requires a shock to the system.

In Part II, we confront three fundamental problems threatening not just MBSR's future, but the transformative potential of secular mindfulness itself. While MBSR serves as our primary lens, as the most structured and widely studied program, these issues infect the entire field:

- Chapter 5 exposes Buddhist Entanglement—the tangled roots between secular mindfulness and Buddhism that create unresolved tensions, compromising both traditions while serving neither fully.

- Chapter 6 confronts One-Dimensional Thinking—how the rush to make mindfulness palatable has stripped it of its revolutionary potential, creating a sanitized version that can do more harm than good.

- Chapter 7 reveals Oligarchic Control—how power has concentrated in the hands of a few, creating hierarchical structures that directly contradict mindfulness's core insights about interconnection and collective wisdom.

You may find yourself becoming defensive. Good. That discomfort signals we're touching something real. Rather than reject these critiques, let them fuel your curiosity. We must face these issues with clear eyes before we can transform them.

This isn't about tearing down mindfulness; it's about saving it. Part III will outline the Open MBSR framework, offering concrete solutions to these challenges. But first we must wake up to the reality of what mindfulness has become. The future of this transformative practice depends on our willingness to face uncomfortable truths.

Are you ready to see what's really happening beneath the surface? Let's begin.

Chapter 5

Buddhist Entanglement

The birth of MBSR was nothing short of a paradigm shift. In 1979, Jon Kabat-Zinn dared to reimagine stress reduction at the University of Massachusetts Medical Center. His goal? To translate mindfulness practices into an approach that could serve people of all backgrounds and beliefs. But revolutions are messy, complicated affairs.

MBSR's early pioneers faced a daunting reality: the absence of a secular mindfulness roadmap. Out of necessity, they turned to the wellspring of Buddhist wisdom. This pragmatic decision would shape the field for decades to come.

What began as temporary scaffolding—Buddhist practices and frameworks borrowed to structure the secular program—became permanently embedded in MBSR's foundation. Teachers embarked on transformative journeys to Buddhist retreats, studied under venerated masters, and steeped themselves in ancient practices. These experiences weren't merely influential; they became the bedrock of the entire movement.

Buddhist institutions evolved into de facto training grounds. Within their walls, aspiring MBSR instructors refined their craft, deepened their understanding, and learned the delicate art of translating profound concepts into accessible practices.

This Buddhist wellspring wasn't a temporary resource. It became a permanent, vital artery feeding the growth of MBSR. Even today, countless teachers draw sustenance from Buddhist retreats, texts, and mentors. It's a living link to mindfulness' ancient roots.

Yet this deep connection created a paradox. How could MBSR establish itself as a secular, medical intervention while maintaining such intimate ties to spiritual traditions? This tension between Buddhist origins and secular applications became a defining challenge for the field.

The entanglement is undeniable. The crucial question is how we navigate it. How do we honor these roots while pushing into uncharted territories? How do we preserve the essence of these teachings while making them truly accessible to all?

This Buddhist influence has profoundly shaped the teaching, study, and integration of mindfulness across various domains. It's simultaneously a source of immense strength and a potential limitation. As we forge ahead, we must confront this reality with clear eyes, finding ways to harness the wisdom of Buddhism without being constrained by it.

The path forward demands nuance and discernment. We must acknowledge our debt to Buddhist traditions while crafting a uniquely secular approach. It's a delicate balancing act between reverence for the past and bold innovation for the future, through which we must:

- Recognize the revolutionary nature of MBSR's origins
- Understand the necessity of early Buddhist influence
- Acknowledge the ongoing impact of Buddhist teachings
- Confront the tension between secular goals and spiritual roots
- Explore ways to honor tradition while fostering innovation
- Seek a balance between accessibility and depth of practice

The story of MBSR is one of adaptation, challenge, and continuous evolution. As we write its next chapters, we must remain mindful of where we've been, clear-eyed about where we are, and boldly imaginative about where we might go. This chapter focuses on the first challenge: Buddhist entanglement. By understanding how MBSR's Buddhist roots both nourish and constrain its growth, we can lay the groundwork for deeper critiques to come. This isn't about tearing down what Jon Kabat-Zinn and others have built. It's about examining our foundation with clear eyes so we can build something even stronger. By understanding these challenges, we lay the groundwork for Open MBSR, an evolution that preserves what works while addressing what doesn't.

Contemplative Sciences: Navigating the Buddhist–Science Intersection

The collision of Buddhism and contemplative science is a potential credibility crisis for MBSR. While not always aimed directly at MBSR, the critiques of this intersection strike at the core of our scientific foundations.

Evan Thompson's book *Why I Am Not a Buddhist* (2020) doesn't mince words. He spotlights the Mind and Life Institute, that collaboration between neuroscientists, philosophers, and the Dalai Lama, as prime evidence of Buddhism's scientific courtship. Thompson warns that this "neural Buddhism" risks infecting our research with bias, subtly nudging us toward predetermined outcomes.

But Thompson's critique is merely the opening salvo. Miguel Farias and Catherine Wikholm dig deeper in *The Buddha Pill: Can Meditation Change You?* (2015). They expose the tangled web of relationships between mindfulness teachers, researchers, and Buddhist institutions. Their message? Beware the echo chamber. This interconnectedness could lead to cherry-picking evidence that confirms our preconceptions about mindfulness benefits, while conveniently ignoring contradictory data.

These critiques aren't meant to diminish the potential of MBSR. They're a clarion call, demanding we confront the complex challenges stemming from our Buddhist roots. The proposed solutions are both sweeping and practical:

- **Embrace methodological rigor:** We need research designs that can withstand the harshest scrutiny.
- **Combat publication bias:** Preregistering research protocols ensures transparency and prevents selective reporting.

- **Report all results:** Negative findings are just as crucial as positive ones. We can't paint a complete picture of mindfulness by hiding half the canvas.
- **Diversify research teams:** Include skeptics. Challenge assumptions. Let different perspectives clash and create sparks of insight.
- **Expand theoretical frameworks:** Don't get trapped in Buddhist concepts. Explore alternative explanations for mindfulness effects.
- **Prioritize transparency:** Disclose connections between researchers and Buddhist or mindfulness organizations. Let readers judge potential influences for themselves.

Addressing these concerns will forge a path forward that balances our Buddhist-inspired roots with unyielding scientific standards. It can create a foundation for Open MBSR that's unshakable, built on diverse perspectives and unbiased inquiry.

This approach elevates the entire field. By embracing these challenges, we enhance the scientific credibility and inclusivity of our practice. We create a mindfulness movement that's not just effective but unassailable in its commitment to truth and transparency.

> **Note:** The intersection of Buddhism and science doesn't have to be an Achilles' heel. With the right approach, it can be our greatest strength. By acknowledging our roots while pushing beyond them, MBSR can create a practice that's deeply grounded and endlessly adaptable.

Stealth Buddhism: The Hidden Roots of MBSR

A tempest brews in the mindfulness world, with Candy Gunther Brown at its eye. Her 2019 book, *Debating Yoga and Mindfulness in Public Schools,* is provocative and potentially revolutionary.

Brown's thesis is a game changer: she claims MBSR and other mindfulness programs are covertly injecting Buddhist ideas into secular spaces, masked as stress reduction techniques. She dubs it "stealth Buddhism," a term that's a direct challenge to mindfulness as we know it.

In point of fact, it represents a clash of ethics, transparency, and the increasingly blurred line between spiritual and secular. In educational settings, Brown argues, mindfulness programs tiptoe dangerously close to breaching the church–state divide. In business and governmental institutions, they risk encroaching on religious freedoms.

Open MBSR's concerns are precise. It's not the practices themselves under fire, but their presentation. The real issues are:

- Concealing Buddhist origins
- Employing Buddhist imagery in secular contexts
- Using Buddhist terminology without explanation
- Subtle "dog whistles" signaling Buddhist connections
- Buddhist-trained instructors leading ostensibly secular programs

These elements are the true Trojan horses of "stealth Buddhism," surreptitiously introducing Buddhist concepts without full disclosure. Brown's critique is incisive, as summarized here:

- Are we deceiving participants about these practices' true nature?
- Are we divorcing mindfulness from its cultural and spiritual heritage?
- Are participants fully informed about what they're engaging in?
- Is this a form of subtle indoctrination? (Brown, 2019)

The coup de grâce? Jon Kabat-Zinn's own admission: "From the beginning of MBSR, I bent over backward to structure it and find ways to speak about it that avoided as much as possible the risk of it being seen as Buddhist, 'New Age,' 'Eastern Mysticism' or just plain 'flakey'"(Kabat-Zinn, 2011, p. 282). This revelation exposes a deliberate strategy of obfuscation, a calculated move that's opened a Pandora's box of ethical quandaries.

Kabat-Zinn's acknowledgment shines a glaring spotlight on MBSR's precarious balancing act between accessibility and integrity. It compels us to grapple with uncomfortable truths about our approach to mindfulness.

This isn't a call to dismantle MBSR. It's a push for evolution. We need a more nuanced, transparent approach to mindfulness in secular spaces, one that honors its Buddhist roots while preserving its secular applicability.

We face a crossroads: Ignore these critiques and risk our credibility, or confront them head-on. We can pioneer new ways of presenting MBSR that are honest about its origins and influences. We can empower participants to make truly informed choices about their engagement with these practices while presenting them free of Buddhist language, symbolization, or subtle indoctrination.

McMindfulness: The Fast Food of Spirituality

In 2011, Buddhist teacher Miles Neale ignited a firestorm in the mindfulness world with a single word: "McMindfulness." The blaze has only grown since, fueled by voices like Ron Purser, whose 2019 book *McMindfulness: How Mindfulness Became the New Capitalist Spirituality* turned a spark into an inferno.

Purser isn't a lone rebel. David Loy, Zack Walsh, and others have joined the uprising, each adding fuel to a growing bonfire of dissent. Their message? Mindfulness has morphed into a Trojan horse, smuggling a diluted version of Buddhism into our lives, its ethical core gutted and repackaged for mass consumption.

The symptoms of this spiritual junk food are everywhere:

- Instant enlightenment apps promising Nirvana between notifications

- Exclusive retreats turning inner peace into a luxury good
- Corporate mindfulness programs sedating workers instead of transforming toxic cultures
- Mindfulness stripped of its Buddhist ethical framework, reduced to a mere commodity

It's a tempting offer: all the benefits of ancient wisdom without the pesky moral obligations or communal responsibilities. But just as a diet of chicken nuggets leaves you malnourished and craving more, this fast-food spirituality fails to satisfy our deepest hunger.

The true danger of McMindfulness isn't just its superficiality, but its potential for harm. By commoditizing mindfulness, we risk losing its essence. The communal aspect withers, replaced by solitary app sessions. The uncomfortable, challenging parts are smoothed away, leaving only the palatable remains. What's left is a fraction of a whole: a practice stripped of its power to transform. In our rush to make mindfulness accessible, we've made it incomplete. We've traded depth for breadth, wisdom for convenience. The irony is palpable: In trying to spread mindfulness far and wide, we may have diluted the very thing that makes it worth spreading.

In the corporate realm, mindfulness becomes a Band-Aid on the gaping wounds of toxic work culture. It's easier to teach employees to breathe through stress than to confront the root causes of burnout and exploitation. Mindfulness becomes an unwitting accomplice in perpetuating the very systems it was meant to challenge.

But here's where we pivot from the standard critique. The villain isn't commercialization itself. It's mindless commercialization. It's the unthinking application of market logic to spiritual practices without considering the consequences.

What if, instead of rejecting capitalism outright, we forged a framework that inherently addresses the ethical concerns of McMindfulness? What if we could harness the market's power, rather than being manipulated by it?

Envision a mindfulness practice as accessible and far-reaching as fast food, but as nourishing as a home-cooked meal. A practice that doesn't shy away from profit, but reinvests that money into deepening and spreading genuine wisdom. A practice that engages with corporations not to pacify workers, but to transform workplaces from within.

This isn't about building a better McDonald's. It's about creating a new model: one that satisfies immediate needs while nourishing our deepest selves. It's about wielding the tools of capitalism not to water down mindfulness, but to amplify its transformative power.

As we chart the course for Open MBSR, these aren't just philosophical musings. They're the blueprint for a mindfulness practice that can thrive in the modern world without losing its soul—a practice as at home in the boardroom as in the meditation hall, not because it's been stripped of its essence, but because it's potent enough to transform any environment it touches.

The goal isn't to make mindfulness popular. It's to make it powerful. To create a practice that doesn't just help us cope with the world as it is, but gives us the tools to reimagine it. A practice as revolutionary as it is accessible, as profound as it is practical. Can we create a mindfulness practice that's both commercially viable and ethically uncompromising? A practice that isn't a luxury for the affluent but a resource for all? That's the challenge before us.

The Spiritual Hustle: Enlightenment for Sale

The modern mindfulness landscape is a wild frontier where Buddhist monks moonlight as life coaches and enlightenment comes with a price tag. It's a world where the line between guru and CEO is as blurry as your mind after a marathon meditation session.

Gone are the days when becoming a Buddhist teacher meant renouncing worldly possessions and adhering to strict ethical codes. Those weren't just arbitrary rules; they were a firewall against the corruption of spiritual authority. But in today's mindfulness gold rush, a new breed of spiritual entrepreneur has found a loophole big enough to drive a semitruck through.

These savvy individuals are masters of the quick-change act: Buddhist teacher by day, mindfulness instructor by night. It's a clever sleight of hand that lets them bypass monastic restrictions while cashing in on their spiritual street cred. They cultivate the deep, trusting relationships of a spiritual teacher without those pesky limits on personal gain.

The implications are staggering. With their "spiritual hat" on, these teachers build a devoted following based on timeless wisdom. Then, faster than you can say "Om," they don their "capitalist hat" and monetize that, following through with an endless stream of books, courses, workshops, retreats, apps, and coaching sessions. It's spiritual authority leveraged for commercial gain, and it's turning the traditional power dynamics of spirituality on its head.

In the old system, checks and balances were baked in. These were safeguards against the abuse of spiritual power:

- Buddhist teachers relied on the generosity of students.
- Hindu gurus offered teachings freely.
- Sufi masters embraced poverty.

But when spirituality goes commercial, all bets are off. The power dynamic shifts dramatically in favor of the teacher. Students feel pressured to pay for "advanced" teachings. Teachers feel compelled to deliver marketable "results" rather than authentic guidance. The sacred teacher–student relationship becomes a transaction, with spiritual growth priced according to market demand.

Even worse, this trend risks creating a spiritual caste system based on economic status. Expensive luxury retreats and exclusive coaching programs become the new markers of "advanced" practice. It's not hard to see parallels with the Catholic Church's sale of indulgences, a practice that became so egregious it sparked the Protestant Reformation.

The situation screams for new ethical frameworks:

- Clear boundaries between traditional Buddhist roles and secular mindfulness instruction
- Transparent guidelines that address the realities of commercial practice

- Structures that ensure equal access to mindfulness teachings, regardless of economic status

Grappling with these issues isn't just navel-gazing for ethicists. It's a compelling case for separating mindfulness practices from their Buddhist origins. This separation would benefit both Buddhism and secular mindfulness. It would preserve the integrity of Buddhist teachings and the traditional teacher–student relationship. Simultaneously, it would allow for the development of a truly secular mindfulness practice with its own ethical framework, free from the complications of mixed spiritual and commercial motivations.

The path forward isn't about demonizing those who teach mindfulness for a living. It's about creating a system where spiritual integrity and economic reality can coexist. It's about building a mindfulness practice that's accessible to all, not just those who can afford the premium package. And it's about ensuring that in our quest for inner peace, we don't lose our moral compass along the way.

The challenge before us is monumental, but so are the stakes. Can we create a mindfulness practice that's economically viable and ethically sound? Can we preserve the depth of ancient wisdom while making it accessible in the modern marketplace? These questions are the key to ensuring that mindfulness remains a transformative force rather than just another consumer product.

But Wait! What About Buddhist Psychology?

In the wild jungle of mindfulness, a new creature has emerged: Buddhist psychology. It's the Frankenstein's monster of spiritual exploration, cobbled together from ancient Eastern wisdom and Western scientific thought. But like many hybrids, it might be more mutant than masterpiece.

This intellectual hybrid emerged in the mid-20th century, with pioneering thinkers playing academic alchemists, fusing Buddhist insights with Freudian theories. The 1970s and 1980s saw this creation truly come alive, thanks to a new generation of scholars and practitioners. These individuals, equally versed in Buddhist meditation and Western psychology, sought to transform spiritual gold into scientific currency.

Today, Buddhist psychology has invaded everything from therapy couches to corporate boardrooms. It's marketed as Buddhism-lite: all the enlightenment, none of the religious baggage. On the surface, it seems like the perfect solution to our mindfulness dilemmas, a way to keep the Buddhist essence while draining away the spiritual excess.

But scratch that shiny surface, and the facade crumbles. Buddhism isn't just a toolbox of stress-reduction techniques; it's a comprehensive worldview, complete with concepts like Karma, rebirth, and enlightenment. Try cramming those into a materialist, empirical framework, and you'll find they fit about as well as a camel through the eye of a needle.

This forced marriage of Eastern spirituality and Western science dilutes Buddhism and compromises the integrity of psychology itself. Cherry-picking Buddhist concepts and slapping psychological labels on them isn't science; it's intellectual sleight of hand. It reduces rich, nuanced spiritual teachings to pop psychology sound bites and risks turning psychology into a watered-down amalgam of mismatched ideas. This approach doesn't elevate either field; instead, it threatens to undermine the credibility of both, creating a hybrid that's neither authentically spiritual nor rigorously scientific.

The problems run deeper:

- **Cultural appropriation:** It's a form of intellectual colonialism where Western paradigms are imposed on Eastern wisdom traditions.
- **False advertising:** It promises the benefits of Buddhism without the spiritual commitments.
- **Compromised integrity:** It waters down both Buddhism and psychology in an attempt to make them compatible.
- **Missed opportunities:** Instead of addressing real challenges in mindfulness, it creates a facade of resolution.

Buddhist psychology's popularity isn't a triumph; it's a smokescreen obscuring mindfulness's real challenges: the spiritual–secular tension, cultural appropriation risks, and the need for ethical frameworks. We must courageously maintain clear boundaries between spiritual and secular, not to build walls, but to create clarity. This respects Buddhist traditions while advancing truly secular well-being approaches.

Moving beyond this illusion opens doors to authentic, innovative mindfulness practices that stand on their own, whether spiritual or secular. The mindfulness movement faces a pivotal choice: Shall it continue diluting traditions, or instead forge a path respecting both ancient wisdom and modern science? This decision will shape how we understand and cultivate well-being. The era of half-measures is over. Now begins the real work of creating authentic, ethical, and effective mindfulness practices.

The Fork in the Road: Derivation Versus Recontextualization

This chapter has dissected the ailments of modern mindfulness—the stealth Buddhism, the spiritual capitalism, the muddled merger of contemplative practices and scientific inquiry. But pointing out problems is child's play. The real challenge is crafting solutions. Enter derivation and recontextualization.

Derivation is evolution unleashed. It's seizing an idea, a practice, or a concept and using it as a launch pad to create something entirely new. It's honoring your roots while having the audacity to outgrow them. *Recontextualization*, however, is more like a transplant. It's plucking something wholesale and dropping it into foreign soil, crossing fingers it'll flourish without altering its core.

At a glance, the outcomes might appear similar. But dig deeper, and the contrasts become glaring. A derived practice is a free spirit, unshackled by its origins, primed to adapt and evolve. It's responsive to new insights, cultural shifts, and scientific breakthroughs. A recontextualized practice, on the other hand, is a prisoner of its history, forever tethered to its source, struggling to truly thrive in its new environment.

Consider this analogy:

- *Derivation* is jazz emerging from blues. It absorbed the soul, the scales, the rhythms of blues and birthed something revolutionary. Jazz acknowledges blues but speaks its own distinct language.
- *Recontextualization* is classical music on synthesizers. Sure, it sounds different, but peel away the electronic facade and it's the same tune, unchanged and stagnant.

In the mindfulness realm, derivation might mean taking mindful breathing and developing entirely new, scientifically validated stress reduction and mental wellness techniques. No ancient doctrines are necessary. Recontextualization? That's teaching traditional Eastern meditation in a corporate setting, just with the spiritual language swapped for business jargon.

For Open MBSR to truly make its mark, it must embrace derivation. It's not about disrespecting its Buddhist roots; it's about honoring them by allowing their wisdom to ignite something new. It's about forging a secular framework that resonates with a diverse, global audience without getting lost in translation.

By choosing derivation, Open MBSR can:

- Acknowledge its Buddhist inspiration without apology
- Adapt techniques to fit a new, secular worldview
- Develop practices that transcend cultural boundaries
- Remain agile, incorporating insights from science and diverse traditions

This isn't just wordplay. It's about the essence of MBSR, about operating from truth, not convenient half-truths. Choosing derivation over recontextualization means choosing authenticity over convenience, innovation over imitation. It's about creating a practice that's resilient, inclusive, and truly universal. The path of derivation isn't easy. It demands creativity, courage, and venturing into uncharted territory. But it leads to a mindfulness practice honest about its past and excited about its future. The choice is stark: Compose something fresh or keep playing the same old melody on new instruments.

Will we have the courage and conviction to derive, to evolve, to create? Or will we settle for forever explaining away the contradictions in our approach? The world craves a mindfulness practice built for today's challenges, not yesterday's. It's time to innovate. The future of mindfulness, authentic, adaptable, and truly transformative, is waiting to be born. We must bring it into existence.

Unpacking the Buddhist DNA: A Blueprint for Transparency

Chapter 3 ripped off the Band-Aid. For the first time in print, the Buddhist skeleton of MBSR has been exposed.

This excavation revealed more than a sprinkling of Eastern spice. It unearthed a full-blown Buddhist blueprint that forms MBSR's very DNA. From the Three Jewels to the Four Noble Truths, from the Four Foundations of Mindfulness to the principle of *ehipassiko*, that chapter traced the Buddhist genes coursing through MBSR's veins.

But I didn't stop at what was included. I also illuminated what was deliberately left on the cutting room floor. Concepts like Karma, rebirth, Nirvana, and other pillars of Buddhism are absent from MBSR. This isn't an oversight; it's a calculated gambit allowing MBSR to walk the tightrope between ancient wisdom and modern secular practice.

By clearly mapping what's been borrowed and what's been left behind, we've created a new launch pad. We're no longer doomed to endless recontextualization of Buddhist practices. Instead, we can now derive from this clearly defined foundation, free to innovate while still honoring the essence of these teachings.

This is a blueprint for mindfulness's future. By grasping MBSR's Buddhist roots with this level of clarity, MBSR can:

- Innovate with integrity, knowing exactly what it's building upon
- Address issues of cultural appropriation head-on
- Create truly secular practices that don't require stealth Buddhism
- Evolve the field in response to new research and societal needs

This is not severing MBSR from its roots, but growing beyond them. This is about crafting a practice as transparent as it is transformative, as secular as it is profound. The path forward is clear: acknowledge our debts, learn from our sources, and dare to innovate. This is a way to set a new standard for adapting ancient wisdom to modern needs.

The future of mindfulness isn't in imitation or obfuscation, but in honest derivation. It's about using the best of Buddhism as a launch pad for something tailored to this time and place. This is mindfulness's moment of truth. Will we continue playing hide-and-seek with our Buddhist roots, or stand in the full light of transparency? The choice will shape not just MBSR's future, but the entire landscape of modern mindfulness. The world is watching.

Siddhartha's Rebellion: A Lesson in Breaking Free

Rewind the clock, not just decades but millennia. Before mindfulness was a buzzword, before MBSR existed, there was Siddhartha Gautama. Born into a Hindu family, he was the golden child of ancient Indian spirituality. Vedic rituals? Mastered. Extreme asceticism? Been there, done that.

But Siddhartha wasn't content with hand-me-down wisdom. He surveyed the spiritual buffet before him and said, "Not good enough." He dared to ask, "What if there's another way?"

This wasn't just a personal crisis of faith. It was a revolution. Siddhartha, later known as the Buddha, didn't just tweak the system. He demolished it. He unleashed a seismic shift against the rigid caste system and ritual-obsessed practices of his day. In their place, he built something new, something that addressed the core of human suffering and the path to liberation.

This act of rebellion, this untethering from tradition, birthed Buddhism. It wasn't a gradual evolution. It was a quantum leap. The Buddha's teachings, the Dharma, ignited and spread like wildfire across Asia. Why? Because they were adaptable, speaking to a Chinese peasant as powerfully as to an Indian scholar.

Now, Open MBSR stands at a similar crossroads. It faces a choice: cling to the comfortable familiarity of its Buddhist roots or follow the Buddha's example and forge its own path?

The Buddha's journey is a blueprint for radical innovation, showing us that respecting roots doesn't mean being shackled by them. It proves that true wisdom isn't about preserving tradition, but addressing real human needs.

Just as the Buddha retained certain Hindu elements while discarding others, Open MBSR has the opportunity—no, the responsibility—to be discerning. This isn't about reinventing the wheel. It's about building a better vehicle for our modern journey, taking what works and having the audacity to innovate beyond it.

The Buddha aimed to address suffering, not start a religion. Open MBSR is about developing a practice that meets the realities of modern life. Our path is innovation, not imitation. We're distilling ancient wisdom to seed something new, tailored to our time. This is our chance to honor the Buddha's rebellious spirit by charting our own course.

The question is: Do we have the courage to face the discomfort of innovation? Or will we hide behind tradition, missing our chance to make a difference? The Buddha didn't play it safe. He dared to imagine a different way. Now it's our turn. Will we rise to the challenge? The future of mindfulness, as authentic, adaptable, and transformative, awaits. We must bring it into existence.

Algebra: The Universal Language Born from Islamic Wisdom

Picture this: ninth-century Persia. Europe's stumbling through the Dark Ages, but in the Islamic world, a mathematical revolution is brewing. Its name? Algebra. Its meaning? "The reunion of broken parts." Its creator, Muhammad ibn Musa al-Khwarizmi, had no clue his "al-jabr" would one day unite the then-fragmented landscape of global mathematics.

Algebra wasn't content to stay within Islamic scholarly walls. It refused confinement. During the Islamic golden age, knowledge wasn't hoarded; it was shared, debated, and refined. Scholars built bridges, connecting ideas from diverse civilizations. This intellectual crucible was the perfect breeding ground for algebra to outgrow its cultural cradle.

Today, while algebra might be the bane of struggling high schoolers, it is more importantly the universal language of quantity and structure. It's the backbone of scientific revolutions, technological breakthroughs, and economic models. From Wall Street to Silicon Valley, from quantum physics to climate science, algebra permeates everything.

Why did algebra succeed where other mathematical systems faltered? The answer lies in its DNA:

- **Abstraction:** Algebra deals with general principles, not culturally specific examples. It's as relevant in Tokyo as in Toronto.
- **Practicality:** It solves real-world problems across disciplines. Bridge building or budget balancing, algebra's got you covered.
- **Universality:** Its concepts are accessible to anyone, anywhere. Numbers don't have an accent.
- **Adaptability:** As new fields emerge, algebra adapts. It's as crucial to AI as it was to ancient astronomy.

For all its global conquest, algebra hasn't forgotten its roots. Every utterance of "algebra" pays homage to its Islamic origins. Yet the word itself is a linguistic fossil, preserving the memory of its birthplace even as it spans the globe. And herein lies a potent idea. If we may use this as a blueprint for ideas transcending origins without erasing them, this becomes mindfulness's roadmap beyond its Buddhist beginnings. Imagine mindfulness mimicking algebra's journey: retaining essence while shedding cultural specificity, becoming as universal as mathematics while honoring its roots.

This isn't cultural appropriation, but proliferation, letting a powerful idea evolve to serve humanity globally. Like algebra emerging from Islamic scholarship to revolutionize mathematics, mindfulness can emerge from Buddhism to transform global mental health. The question isn't whether mindfulness can make this leap, but whether we have the vision and courage to see it through. Can we create a practice as universal as algebra?

The path is clear but challenging. It requires shedding attachments to tradition and embracing innovation's discomfort. This is our moment. We can cling to familiar Buddhist shores or sail uncharted waters. Will we transform mindfulness into a global language of mental well-being, as revolutionary and universal as algebra?

Beyond Buddhist Entanglement

Buddhist entanglement isn't just a historical footnote: It's the first critical fault line threatening MBSR's foundation. This chapter has peeled back the layers to expose a complex web of challenges:

- Stealth Buddhism is undermining secular credibility.
- McMindfulness is diluting transformative potential.
- The spiritual hustle is corrupting teacher–student relationships.
- Buddhist psychology is creating a false synthesis.

At the same time that this deep examination has revealed challenging problems, it has conversely illuminated a path forward through derivation rather than recontextualization. Like algebra emerging from Islamic scholarship to become a universal language of mathematics, mindfulness can transcend its Buddhist origins while honoring its roots.

> **Key Takeaways**
>
> - Transparency beats stealth; we must be honest about our origins.
> - Innovation trumps imitation; we need new forms, not just new packaging.
> - Integrity demands clarity; secular practice needs clear boundaries.
> - Evolution requires courage; we must dare to create something new.
> - The path ahead demands more than just resolving Buddhist entanglement. It requires fundamentally reimagining how we think about, teach, and practice mindfulness.

Reflection Questions

1. What becomes possible when mindfulness is truly freed from religious entanglement?
2. How might secular practice maintain depth without spiritual dependency?
3. What new forms of practice might emerge from honest derivation?

Looking Ahead

The revolution begins with clear seeing. Now that you've confronted Buddhist entanglement, you're ready to examine how one-dimensional thinking has further compromised mindfulness's potential. The journey of critique continues, but each step brings you closer to genuine transformation.

Chapter 6

Beyond Black and White

In the grand tapestry of human thought, we often find ourselves drawn to simple answers, to clean lines and clear divisions. It's a comforting illusion, this idea that the world can be neatly categorized into black and white, right and wrong, us and them. But reality, in all its messy glory, refuses to conform to our desire for simplicity.

This chapter delves into the treacherous waters of one-dimensional thinking, exploring how our brain's preference for simplicity can lead us astray, particularly in the realm of mindfulness and personal growth. I'll unpack the neuroscience behind cognitive biases, examine the pitfalls of politicizing mindfulness, and confront the shadow aspects of our psyche that we so often try to ignore.

But this isn't just a critique of our mental shortcomings. It's an invitation to embrace a more nuanced, dialectical approach to thinking and living. Building on the insights from Acceptance and Commitment Therapy (ACT) explored in Chapter 4, this chapter explains how essential it is to embrace paradox.

To help you navigate this journey, I draw inspiration from thinkers as diverse as Herbert Marcuse and Carl Jung, from the ancient wisdom of Eastern philosophy to the cutting-edge insights of modern neuroscience. I challenge you to hold contradictions, to sit with discomfort, and to find unity in apparent opposites.

This exploration serves as a roadmap for evolving MBSR into a more robust, flexible, and holistic practice. It aims to transform MBSR into an approach that doesn't shy away from complexity but rather embraces it as the very essence of human experience.

This exploration includes:

- The treacherous waters of one-dimensional thinking
- The neuroscience behind cognitive biases
- The pitfalls of politicizing mindfulness
- The shadow aspects of our psyche
- The potential of dialectical thinking

Set aside your preconceptions and step into the rich, multidimensional landscape of human consciousness. It's time to think beyond the binary, to see the world not in black and white, but in all its vibrant, sometimes contradictory hues.

One-Dimensional Thinking

In the realm of modern thought, one-dimensional thinking stands as a concept both prescient and enduring. Herbert Marcuse, in his 1964 work "One-Dimensional Man," unveiled a critique of advanced industrial society that resonates powerfully today. Marcuse, a German American philosopher of the Frankfurt School, identified a troubling trend within postwar Western prosperity: the flattening of discourse and erosion of critical thought.

Beneath the facade of freedom and choice in modern capitalist societies, Marcuse uncovered a form of social control more insidious than overt oppression. This control operated through fabricated needs, co-opting potential opposition and promoting a mode of thought incapable of challenging the status quo. One-dimensional thinking collapsed complex realities into simple, digestible concepts, rejected contradiction, and closed off discourse to ideas that might shake the foundations of the existing order.

To grasp the full implications of one-dimensional thinking today, I must expand on Marcuse's original formulation. It now represents a mode of cognition that shuns complexity, nuance, and contradiction. It manifests as linear, absolutist thinking, seeking simple solutions to complex problems. This expanded concept shows itself in black-and-white views, favoring standardized approaches over contextual understanding and resisting critical examination of core assumptions.

One-dimensional thinking often masquerades as positive simplification, offering clear guidelines promising desired outcomes. But this apparent clarity exacts a steep price. By reducing complex realities to simple maxims or techniques, it strips practices and ideas of their depth, nuance, and transformative potential.

This tendency becomes especially problematic when applied to personal growth, mental health, and societal change. Consider these specific manifestations:

- **Uncritical acceptance of positive attitudes:** Modern mindfulness and well-being practices often promote supposedly universally positive attitudes like nonjudging, patience, acceptance, or gratitude, while beneficial, one-dimensional thinking fails to critically examine their potential downsides or contexts where they might backfire. Extreme nonjudging could lead to moral relativism or failure to discern harm. Misapplied acceptance might breed complacency in the face of injustice or personal stagnation.

- **Ideological alignment and simplification of complex issues:** One-dimensional thinking often links personal growth practices with specific political and social stances, reducing complex societal issues to simple, "correct" positions. Mindfulness practices might become uncritically tied to particular dietary choices, environmental activism, or social justice approaches. While not inherently problematic, the danger lies in presenting them as a package deal, where adopting one practice implies subscribing to an entire set of beliefs and lifestyle choices.

- **Closed systems of thought and lack of debate:** Perhaps most concerning is the creation of closed thought systems where alternative viewpoints or critiques are unwelcome.

This manifests as a lack of genuine debate within communities centered on specific practices or philosophies. When practitioners or teachers resist engaging with critical perspectives or questioning fundamental assumptions, it creates Marcuse's "universe of closed discourse." In such an environment, the practice or philosophy risks becoming dogmatic, losing the capacity for self-reflection and evolution.

- **Loss of paradox and complexity:** Many contemplative and philosophical traditions historically embraced paradox and complexity as essential elements of wisdom. However, in modern, popularized forms, these practices often lose this nuanced approach for more straightforward, prescriptive methods. This simplification, while increasing accessibility, risks stripping practices of their deeper transformative potential. The ability to hold contradictory ideas in tension, embrace uncertainty, and engage with the full complexity of human experience is often sacrificed for easily digestible, marketable techniques.

- **Resistance to critique:** One-dimensional thinking often manifests as resistance to critique or defensiveness toward questioning. This appears in communities or schools of thought reacting dismissively or hostilely to outside criticism or internal questioning. Such resistance reflects a tendency to reject or ignore ideas that don't fit the established framework, leading to intellectual stagnation and failure to adapt to new insights or changing circumstances.

The impact of one-dimensional thinking in these contexts runs deep. It commoditizes well-being, reducing complex human experiences to products or services for sale. It standardizes practices, ignoring individual and cultural differences. Most critically, it undermines the very goals of personal and societal transformation these practices aim to achieve, promoting adaptation to existing conditions rather than fostering genuine, critical engagement with oneself and society.

Recognizing these pitfalls of one-dimensional thinking is crucial for anyone engaged in or studying practices aimed at personal growth, mental health, or societal change. It challenges people to approach these practices with a more nuanced, critical eye, to embrace complexity and contradiction, and to remain open to ongoing questioning and evolution. Only by transcending one-dimensional thinking can we hope to unlock the full, transformative potential of these powerful practices and philosophies.

Why Our Brains Prefer Simplicity

The human brain, a marvel of intense, almost unimaginable complexity, paradoxically craves simplicity. This inclination toward one-dimensional thinking, marked by oversimplification and binary perspectives, is deeply woven into our neural fabric. Unraveling the science behind this tendency can illuminate why we default to simplistic views and, crucially, how we might cultivate more nuanced cognition.

At the heart of our cognitive processes lies a fundamental duality, articulated by Daniel Kahneman in *Thinking, Fast and Slow* (2011). Kahneman identifies two thinking systems:

- System 1 is rapid, intuitive, and emotional.
- System 2 is slower, more deliberative, and logical.

Our brain's preference for System 1 in daily life often leads us down the path of least resistance, prioritizing quick, efficient processing over deep, nuanced analysis. While this preference serves us well for rapid decision-making, it significantly contributes to one-dimensional thinking.

Lisa Feldman Barrett's research on the brain's predictive nature offers further insight (Barrett and Simmons, 2015). She posits that our brains constantly make predictions based on past experiences, a process that can lead to oversimplified interpretations of complex situations. This predictive mechanism, while efficient, can trap us in familiar thought patterns, reinforcing one-dimensional perspectives.

The social nature of our brains also shapes our cognitive tendencies. Matthew D. Lieberman's work (2013) on the Default Mode Network (DMN) reveals how this neural network, active during rest and introspection, contributes to our social cognition. While crucial for navigating our social world, the DMN can also facilitate stereotyping and oversimplification of complex social issues, further entrenching one-dimensional thinking patterns.

Michael Gazzaniga's research on split-brain patients unveils another fascinating aspect of our cognitive architecture (Gazzaniga, 2011). Gazzaniga's work suggests that the left hemisphere acts as an "interpreter," creating coherent narratives even when presented with incomplete or contradictory information. This interpretive function, while essential for making sense of our world, can sometimes lead to oversimplified explanations of complex phenomena, reinforcing one-dimensional perspectives.

Emotional states, particularly stress, can exacerbate our tendency toward simplistic thinking. Robert Sapolsky's extensive research demonstrates how stress impairs the prefrontal cortex, crucial for complex thinking and decision-making (Sapolsky, 2017). Under stress, we default to reflexive, less nuanced cognitive processes. Similarly, Joseph LeDoux's work (2015) on the amygdala and fear processing shows how emotional arousal can trigger rapid, instinctive responses, often resulting in black-and-white thinking, especially in emotionally charged situations.

From an evolutionary standpoint, one-dimensional thinking may have been adaptive. In ancestral environments, quick, simplified thinking patterns were often necessary for survival. The cognitive cost of complex, nuanced thinking may have outweighed its benefits in many everyday situations. Robert Kurzban's work (2012) on the modularity of mind supports this view, suggesting our cognitive architecture evolved to prioritize efficiency over complexity in many scenarios.

Our brain's reward system also reinforces simplistic thinking patterns. Wolfram Schultz's research on dopamine signaling demonstrates how our reward system reinforces behaviors and thought patterns that have led to positive outcomes in the past (Schultz, 2015). This creates a bias toward familiar, simplified thinking patterns that have been previously rewarded, further entrenching one-dimensional perspectives.

Neuroscience reveals several key factors contributing to our tendency toward one-dimensional thinking:

- **Dual processing:** Our brain's preference for fast, intuitive thinking over slower, more deliberative processing
- **Predictive processing:** The brain's tendency to make quick predictions based on past experiences, potentially oversimplifying complex situations
- **Social cognition:** The Default Mode Network's role in facilitating stereotyping and oversimplifying social issues
- **Narrative creation:** The left hemisphere's function as an "interpreter," sometimes leading to oversimplified explanations of complex phenomena
- **Stress response:** The impairment of complex thinking under stress, leading to more reflexive, less nuanced cognitive processes
- **Evolutionary adaptations:** The historical advantage of quick, simplified thinking for survival in ancestral environments
- **Reward reinforcement:** The brain's tendency to reinforce thinking patterns that have led to positive outcomes in the past

Understanding these neurological factors can help us recognize and potentially overcome our tendencies toward one-dimensional thinking.

Despite these ingrained tendencies, hope exists for developing more nuanced thinking. The brain's plasticity offers the potential for change. Through targeted practices and cognitive training, we can strengthen neural pathways associated with analytical and critical thinking.

> **Note:** Mindfulness practices have been shown to enhance activity in the prefrontal cortex and reduce amygdala reactivity, potentially countering some of the neurological bases of one-dimensional thinking.

Understanding the neuroscience behind one-dimensional thinking is a crucial step toward developing strategies to promote more nuanced, multidimensional cognitive approaches. While our brains may default to simplicity, they also possess the remarkable ability to adapt and grow. By leveraging this plasticity, we can work toward cultivating more complex and flexible thinking patterns, both in ourselves and in educational and developmental contexts.

The journey from one-dimensional to multidimensional thinking isn't about completely overriding our brain's natural tendencies. It's about developing awareness of these tendencies and consciously engaging in practices that encourage more nuanced perspectives. As we continue to unravel the complexities of the human brain, we gain valuable tools for fostering cognitive flexibility and depth of understanding, essential qualities in navigating our increasingly complex world.

Mindfulness as a Political Tool?

Welcome to the mindfulness loyalty test, where your awakening comes with required political allegiances. What began as a practice of radical self-inquiry has devolved into an ideological screening tool. The meditation cushion, once a space for unfettered exploration, now doubles as a party membership booth.

Look around your mindfulness communities, centers, and classes. Notice how certain views come preinstalled, like unnecessary software on a new computer. Social justice isn't explored—it's prescribed. Cultural perspectives aren't investigated—they're enforced. Identity politics isn't examined—it's assumed. A practice meant to help you see clearly has become clouded by ideological prerequisites.

In the rush to make mindfulness "progressive," we've created something profoundly regressive: a practice where conformity masquerades as consciousness, and where ideological purity matters more than genuine inquiry.

This isn't some modern misstep. It's history repeating itself, a warning ignored. John Stuart Mill saw it coming. In *On Liberty*, he cautioned us about the tyranny of prevailing opinion (Mill, 1859). Now we're living it, cloaked in the false robes of awareness and acceptance.

Mill's "despotism of custom" isn't just alive—it's thriving in the echo chambers we call mindfulness communities. Where Mill saw societal pressure crushing diverse thought, we now have the soft tyranny of political conformity, all in spaces meant for open awareness. The irony would be laughable if it weren't so damaging.

Mill insisted that engaging with opposing viewpoints was essential. He believed that truly understanding and defending our positions against criticism is crucial for genuine conviction. Yet in many mindfulness circles today, a curious pattern emerges: When core assumptions are questioned, the response often comes wrapped in gentle acknowledgments and compassionate redirects. Like a skillful aikido master, objections are met not with resistance but with a soft smile and a subtle pivot that leaves the fundamental challenge politely unaddressed. The preaching of "nonjudgmental awareness" becomes, ironically, a sophisticated way to sidestep substantive debate.

This ideological entrenchment is misguided and dangerous. We're not facing a simple problem; we're staring down a multiheaded hydra of issues:

- **The mindfulness bubble:** Once open spaces for exploration have transformed into ideological fortresses, where challenging thoughts are treated as invading armies rather than opportunities for growth.
- **Performative enlightenment:** The practice becomes a badge to be displayed, a signal of virtue rather than a path to genuine self-discovery.

- **The activist's meditation:** Personal development and political maneuvering blur into an indistinguishable mess, diluting the power of both.
- **Mindfulness:** Corporations co-opt the practice, packaging it with trendy social initiatives, further cementing its political associations and draining its authenticity.
- **The ideological monastery:** Mindfulness becomes part of a larger ideological lifestyle, creating invisible barriers that keep out diverse perspectives and experiences.

The irony is thick enough to cut with a knife. In our zealous pursuit of inclusivity, we've become the very thing we sought to transcend: exclusive, judgmental, and blind to our own biases. We've taken a practice that could unite humanity in its shared experience of suffering and turned it into yet another wedge driving us apart.

But all is not lost. The path back to genuine mindfulness is still there, obscured but not erased. It begins with a return to these fundamentals:

- **Universal suffering, universal solution:** Stress, pain, and anxiety don't care about your politics. Neither should the practices that help you work with them.
- **Critical compassion:** Foster an environment where empathy and critical thinking coexist. Question everything, especially your own cherished beliefs.
- **Mental diversity:** Create spaces where different thoughts aren't just tolerated, but celebrated. Growth happens at the edges of comfort, not in its center.
- **Bridge-building awareness:** Use mindfulness to transcend divides, not entrench them further. It's a tool for understanding, not a weapon for ideological warfare.
- **Reclaim the secular:** Strip away the political baggage and return to the essence of the practice: awareness, presence, and genuine nonjudgment.

The stakes couldn't be higher. By politicizing mindfulness, we're losing a powerful tool for personal transformation and turning it into a catalyst for further division. We're alienating vast swathes of humanity from a practice that could benefit all, turning a potential solution into part of the problem.

Consider the "us versus them" mentality that pervades our discourse. Mindfulness, at its core, offers an antidote to this toxic thinking. It encourages us to observe our thoughts and judgments without attachment, including those related to political beliefs. But when mindfulness becomes a political football, it inherits the very divisive mentality it's meant to transcend.

This hijacking fundamentally warps the nature of mindfulness. At its essence, mindfulness is about cultivating awareness, compassion, and understanding, qualities that transcend political divisions. By making it a tool of political identity, we're turning a unifying force into a dividing one.

The universality of suffering and the potential of mindfulness to address it cannot be overstated. Stress, anxiety, and pain don't care about your political leanings. By politicizing mindfulness, we risk denying its benefits to those who might need it most, simply because they don't align with the "right" ideological stance.

But there's hope. Recognizing the trap is the first step to escaping it. We have the power to reclaim mindfulness, to restore it as a force for unity rather than division.

Imagine a world where mindfulness serves as common ground, a shared language transcending political boundaries. Where people from all walks of life come together, not despite their differences, but because of them. Where the practice becomes a catalyst for understanding, empathy, and genuine dialogue.

This isn't a utopian fantasy. I believe it's part of the original promise of mindfulness. And it's a promise we can still fulfill.

The path forward isn't easy. It demands courage to challenge our assumptions, humility to admit our biases, and wisdom to see beyond the immediate gratification of ideological alignment.

But the rewards are immeasurable. A mindfulness practice unchained from political dogma. A tool for genuine personal growth and societal healing. A way to navigate the complexities of modern life without succumbing to its divisive forces.

The choice is ours. Will we continue to use mindfulness as a political pawn, or will we reclaim it as a universal birthright? Will we use it to build walls or to build bridges?

The world doesn't need more division. It needs practices that remind us of our shared humanity. Mindfulness, in its purest form, offers exactly that. It's time we returned to that purity, not for the sake of any political ideology, but for the sake of our collective well-being.

The Shadow: Seeing the Whole

Carl Jung's shadow concept illuminates the profound impact of one-dimensional thinking on our mental stability and self-awareness. This exploration reveals how simplistic thinking patterns, marked by both rigid perspectives and underlying fragility when challenged, can obstruct our relationship with our shadow self and, consequently, our overall psychological well-being.

Jung's individual shadow encompasses those parts of ourselves we repress, deny, or remain oblivious to: often the aspects we deem unacceptable or conflicting with our conscious self-image. One-dimensional thinking, characterized by oversimplification and binary views, significantly hinders our ability to recognize and integrate these shadow aspects.

This simplistic thinking affects our shadow relationship in key ways:

- **Denial of complexity:** This encourages simplistic self-views, making it difficult to acknowledge contradictory personality aspects.
- **Increased projection:** This leads to projecting disowned traits onto others, resulting in a polarized worldview.
- **Moral rigidity:** Creating an inflexible moral code complicates acceptance of morally ambiguous shadow aspects.

- **Resistance to change:** This fosters a false sense of self-certainty, challenging engagement in fluid shadow work.

The interplay between one-dimensional thinking and neglected shadow work profoundly impacts mental stability. As the chasm between our conscious self-image and our disowned shadow aspects widens, cognitive dissonance intensifies. This rigid adherence to a simplified self-image creates a fragile psychological state, leading to significant emotional distress and instability when confronted with aspects that don't fit this rigid view.

Emotionally repressed shadow elements emerge during moments of stress or vulnerability, causing unexpected outbursts or out-of-character behaviors. This unpredictability exposes the fragility beneath the rigid exterior, destabilizing both individuals and their relationships. People often feel bewildered by their own actions when shadow aspects suddenly pierce their carefully constructed personas.

In mindfulness and MBSR contexts, one-dimensional thinking manifests problematically:

- **Spiritual bypassing:** Misusing nonjudgmental awareness to avoid confronting difficult emotions or personal issues
- **Toxic positivity:** Overemphasizing constant positivity, hindering acknowledgment of negative experiences
- **Conflict avoidance:** Misinterpreting acceptance as justification for avoiding necessary conflicts or difficult conversations
- **Performative perfection:** Putting on a serene act while suppressing our messy humanity

The rigid pursuit of idealized mindfulness can mask a fragile understanding, leading to perfectionism and harsh self-judgment when falling short of unrealistic standards. This rigidity creates a fragile separation between one's "mindful self" and the rest of life, complicating the integration of practice insights into daily living.

When these one-dimensional thinking patterns permeate a community or movement, they spawn a collective shadow affecting the entire group. Mindfulness communities may develop shared blind spots, collectively ignoring or dismissing critiques or uncomfortable truths about their practices. Rigid adherence to certain interpretations or practices can create a thinly fragile group identity, resistant to criticism and prone to defensive reactions when challenged. This can breed unacknowledged elitism or exclusivity, with the group viewing itself as more enlightened than others.

Unexamined shadow elements might also foster unhealthy power dynamics, placing teachers or leaders on pedestals and allowing potential power abuses to go unchecked. Cultural appropriation issues may arise, where deeper cultural and spiritual contexts of mindfulness practices are ignored or superficially adopted.

> **Note:** Recognizing one-dimensional thinking's impact on our shadow relationship is the first step toward a more integrated, psychologically stable approach to mindfulness and personal growth. By embracing complexity, acknowledging our full range of experiences and emotions, and engaging in honest self-reflection, we can begin integrating our shadow aspects.

For mindfulness practitioners and teachers, moving toward integration might involve:

- Encouraging critical thinking alongside nonjudgmental awareness
- Creating space for expressing and exploring difficult emotions
- Acknowledging mindfulness practices' limitations and potential pitfalls
- Fostering open dialogue and constructive criticism within mindfulness communities
- Integrating shadow work techniques into mindfulness practices

By embracing complexity and encouraging critical thinking, we can cultivate a more flexible and resilient mindfulness approach, better equipped to acknowledge and integrate shadow aspects. This holistic approach works toward a grounded mindfulness practice that acknowledges human experience's full complexity. Such integration not only supports individual mental stability but also contributes to healthier, more authentic mindfulness communities and movements.

In embracing our shadow and transcending one-dimensional thinking's rigidity and fragility, we unlock genuine self-understanding and transformative growth. This journey demands courage and persistence, but the rewards—a more integrated self, deeper relationships, and authentic life engagement—are immeasurable. As we explore and integrate our shadow aspects, we cultivate a richer, more nuanced understanding of ourselves and the world, paving the way for true mental stability and personal evolution.

Dialectical Thinking

As I've unraveled the pitfalls of one-dimensional thinking in mindfulness practices and their politicization, a potent remedy emerges: dialectical thinking. This approach offers a path beyond binary perspectives, cultivating a more nuanced, inclusive, and transformative engagement with mindfulness and the world at large.

Dialectical thinking is a mode of reasoning that embraces paradox, contradiction, and the dynamic interplay of opposing forces. Unlike one-dimensional thinking's stark, either–or view, dialectical thinking recognizes that truth often resides in the synthesis of seemingly contradictory ideas. It allows us to hold multiple perspectives simultaneously, acknowledging the complexity and interdependence of various viewpoints.

In mindfulness and personal growth, dialectical thinking empowers practitioners to:

- Embrace both acceptance and change
- Recognize the coexistence of strength and vulnerability

- Navigate the tension between individual needs and collective responsibilities
- Appreciate the interplay between structure and flexibility in practice

This nuanced approach addresses many challenges identified in the politicization and one-dimensional application of mindfulness practices.

Dialectical thinking's roots run deep in both Eastern and Western philosophical traditions, underscoring its universal relevance and timeless wisdom.

In Eastern philosophy, the Taoist concept of yin and yang exemplifies dialectical thinking. These complementary forces are not opposites in conflict, but interconnected aspects of a greater whole. Each contains the seed of the other, illustrating the continuous flow and transformation that characterize existence. This perspective helps mindfulness practitioners embrace the full spectrum of their experiences, rather than rigidly categorizing them as "positive" or "negative."

Buddhism's Middle Way offers a path of moderation that avoids extremes. This inherently dialectical approach teaches that wisdom and enlightenment lie in finding balance and harmony, rather than adhering to rigid extremes. For mindfulness practitioners, the Middle Way guides a more balanced approach to practice, avoiding both overzealous adherence and complete dismissal of structure.

In Western philosophy, Heraclitus introduced the "unity of opposites," observing that the world is in constant flux and opposites are interconnected and dependent on one another. This understanding helps mindfulness practitioners embrace change and impermanence, rather than rigidly clinging to fixed states or ideas.

The Socratic method embodies dialectical thinking through dialogue, questioning, and critical examination of ideas. This approach encourages intellectual humility and continuous self-examination, qualities that enhance mindfulness practice by fostering genuine curiosity and openness to new perspectives.

Plato formalized the dialectical method as a systematic approach to uncovering truth, typically following a pattern of thesis, antithesis, and synthesis. This process of identifying and reconciling contradictions can guide mindfulness practitioners in navigating complex ethical and philosophical questions without resorting to oversimplification.

Neuroscience reveals that while binary thinking may be our default mode, the brain is capable of more sophisticated, dialectical thinking. The prefrontal cortex plays a key role, allowing for the integration of multiple perspectives and complex factors. Cognitive flexibility, crucial for dialectical thinking, can be developed through practice. Activities that challenge the brain, such as problem-solving, critical thinking, and mindfulness practices, enhance this flexibility.

Dialectical thinking offers solutions to many issues identified with respect to one-dimensional approaches to mindfulness:

- **Overcoming politicization:** By embracing multiple perspectives, dialectical thinking helps depoliticize mindfulness practices.
- **Enhancing critical thinking:** It encourages questioning and critical examination, countering uncritical acceptance of ideas.
- **Navigating complexity:** It equips practitioners to deal with real-world complexities, avoiding oversimplification.
- **Balancing the individual and the collective:** It strikes a balance between personal growth and social responsibility.
- **Fostering inclusivity:** By acknowledging diverse perspectives, it creates more inclusive mindfulness communities.

Applying dialectical thinking to mindfulness practices and communities can lead to more dynamic, inclusive, and transformative environments:

- **Encouraging dialogue:** It fosters open exchange of ideas, valuing diverse perspectives.

- **Embracing paradox:** Communities can hold seemingly contradictory ideas simultaneously.
- **Adaptive growth:** It enables evolution and adaptation without losing touch with foundational principles.
- **Ethical navigation:** It provides a framework for navigating complex ethical issues with nuance.
- **Bridging divides:** By recognizing interconnectedness of opposing viewpoints, it can bridge ideological divides.

Dialectical thinking offers a powerful antidote to the challenges posed by one-dimensional approaches to mindfulness. By embracing complexity, fostering cognitive flexibility, and drawing on ancient wisdom traditions, we can cultivate a more nuanced, inclusive, and transformative approach to mindfulness practice. This not only enhances individual growth but also contributes to the development of vibrant, resilient communities capable of navigating our modern world's complexities.

What does this look like in terms of practical application? To ensure that MBSR remains relevant and sustainable, integrating dialectical thinking is crucial. This approach balances traditional mindfulness's contemplative elements with everyday life's practical realities, addressing many of these challenges.

The following sections discuss ways to weave dialectical thinking into MBSR's fabric.

Elevating Dialectical Thinking as the Tenth Attitude

The cornerstone of this transformation is recognizing dialectical thinking as MBSR's tenth attitude. This new perspective emphasizes embracing complexity, balancing opposing forces, and navigating paradoxes mindfully and in an integrative way. By explicitly incorporating dialectical thinking, we shift the entire practice paradigm. This addition grounds the attitudes in everyday life, relationships, and broader societal contexts, transcending purely monastic or detached mindsets.

Reframing Existing Attitudes Through a Dialectical Lens

With dialectical thinking as a core attitude, we must reframe existing MBSR attitudes through this new perspective. This prevents dangerous misinterpretations and ensures practitioners apply these attitudes in a balanced way, fostering personal growth and healthy relationships. For example, we must:

- Balance acceptance with active change, recognizing that accepting reality doesn't preclude improvement efforts.
- Pair non-striving with purposeful action, acknowledging that while we practice nonattachment to outcomes, we still fully engage in life.
- Complement the beginner's mind with experiential wisdom, valuing fresh perspectives and accumulated knowledge.

Encouraging Reflective Dialectic Practice

To deepen dialectical thinking integration, encourage practitioners to engage in reflective practices focused on identifying and integrating opposing forces within themselves. Structured journaling prompts can guide individuals to explore personal contradictions, helping them recognize and reconcile conflicting aspects of their personalities or experiences. Guided meditations focusing on embracing paradox can provide experiential understanding of dialectical concepts. Group discussions delving into the dialectical nature of common life experiences can normalize internal contradictions and foster shared humanity.

These practices help individuals develop a more nuanced understanding of themselves and their experiences, fostering personal growth and resilience. Regular engagement in such reflective practices cultivates a more flexible, adaptive mindset.

Enhancing Facilitator Training

For effective integration of dialectical thinking into MBSR, teachers and facilitators must be skilled in guiding participants to explore and embrace this approach. This involves comprehensive training in helping students navigate complex discussions and recognize the value of opposing viewpoints.

Facilitators need strategies to avoid oversimplification or polarization in mindfulness practice, instead guiding participants toward more nuanced understanding. Moreover, teachers should learn to model dialectical thinking in their own teaching and practice. This might involve demonstrating how to hold seemingly contradictory ideas simultaneously or approaching challenging situations with both acceptance and readiness for change. By embodying these skills, facilitators more effectively guide their students toward a dialectical mindset.

Fostering Community Dialogue

Creating a community culture that celebrates diverse viewpoints and encourages open, respectful dialogue is crucial for integrating dialectical thinking.

- Establish regular forums or discussion groups through which differing perspectives are actively sought and explored.
- Implement practices that encourage deep listening and perspective-taking, fostering empathy and understanding among community members.
- Develop guidelines for constructive disagreement and dialogue to create a safe space for exploring diverse viewpoints.

These guidelines might include principles of respectful communication, active listening, and commitment to seeking understanding rather than winning arguments. Such an environment prevents echo chambers and promotes a more balanced, inclusive community, addressing many concerns about mindfulness politicization. This can apply not only to the community of practitioners but act as a model for mindful dialogue in broader social contexts.

Implementing Skeptical Inquiry in Stewardship

At the organizational level, implement skeptical inquiry as a cornerstone of MBSR stewardship and governance.

- Regularly critically evaluate the program's evolution, ensuring it remains true to core principles while adapting to new insights and societal changes.
- Prioritize transparency in decision-making processes, allowing community members to understand and engage with the program's development.
- Actively seek out and engage with program critiques, demonstrating commitment to growth and improvement. Invite external reviews, conduct regular participant and teacher surveys, or host open forums for feedback and discussion.
- Maintain openness to new evidence and perspectives, ensuring MBSR remains dynamic and responsive to emerging research and societal needs.

By maintaining skeptical inquiry at the leadership level, the community safeguards against dogmatism, polarization, and personality cults. This approach ensures the program remains grounded in evidence-based practices while evolving to meet practitioners' changing needs.

Integrating dialectical thinking into MBSR's core equips individuals with cognitive tools to navigate an increasingly complex world. This approach fosters mental flexibility and resilience, allowing practitioners to engage more effectively with the nuances of human experience.

> **Note:** As you move forward, embrace the tension between opposing forces, foster critical engagement alongside acceptance, and create space for diverse perspectives. This journey may challenge you, but it's precisely in this space of tension and exploration that profound growth occurs.

By centering dialectical thinking in MBSR, we foster a more sophisticated approach to understanding ourselves and the world. This has the potential to transform individual lives and contribute to a more nuanced, compassionate, and understanding society. Through this balanced perspective, MBSR can harness mindfulness's transformative power while maintaining commitment to intellectual honesty, ethical conduct, and scientific rigor.

The integration of dialectical thinking into MBSR represents not just an evolution of the practice, but a shift from the current norm in how we approach personal growth and societal change. It offers a path to a more balanced, inclusive, and effective form of mindfulness—one well-equipped to meet our modern world's complex challenges.

Embracing the Full Spectrum

As you conclude this exploration beyond black-and-white thinking, realize that this isn't merely an intellectual exercise—it's a fundamental shift in how you engage with mindfulness, yourself, and the world.

Key Takeaways

- Our brains naturally default to simplicity, even when reality demands nuance.

- One-dimensional thinking has transformed mindfulness from a tool of liberation into an instrument of conformity.

- Shadow aspects don't disappear when ignored, they grow stronger and more influential.

- Dialectical thinking offers a way to hold seemingly contradictory truths like acceptance and change, structure and flexibility.

> - Shadow integration provides a path to wholeness through acknowledging our full humanity.
> - Critical engagement ensures mindfulness remains vital through questioning assumptions and examining blind spots.
>
> These insights lay crucial groundwork for Open MBSR, challenging us to create:
>
> - Teaching approaches that embrace complexity without creating confusion
> - Practice frameworks that acknowledge shadow without getting lost in it
> - Community structures that foster critical thinking while maintaining cohesion

Reflection Questions

1. How can you develop the capacity to hold paradox in your personal practice and teaching?
2. What shadows in your own practice or teaching need acknowledgment and integration?
3. Where might your attachment to certainty be limiting your growth and understanding?
4. How can you foster communities that embrace both critical thinking and connection?

Looking Ahead

As the book turns to examine power structures within mindfulness institutions, these tools of dialectical thinking and shadow integration become essential. They offer not just critique but a path toward genuine transformation: one that acknowledges the full spectrum of human experience. The revolution in mindfulness isn't about replacing one rigid system with another. It's about creating space for the full richness of human experience, in all its messy, beautiful complexity.

The next chapter reveals why this matters more than ever as we confront the oligarchic structures that have come to dominate mindfulness teaching and practice. The journey beyond black-and-white thinking has equipped you with the tools needed to understand and transform these power dynamics.

Chapter 7

Oligarchy: The Hidden Hand

In the hushed halls of meditation centers and behind the scenes at mindfulness retreats, an invisible force shapes who can access ancient wisdom and how it's taught. This force isn't spiritual insight or scientific evidence: It is elite power.

The mindfulness movement faces a paradox: Practices meant to liberate us from suffering have become trapped in systems that perpetuate inequality and privilege. While mindfulness preaches nonattachment and ego dissolution, this movement has also created new hierarchies, new forms of spiritual materialism, and new barriers to access.

This phenomenon goes beyond organizational politics: It determines who gets to define mindfulness, who can teach it, and ultimately, who can benefit from it. The concentration of power in the mindfulness world has created:

- **Economic gatekeeping:** Where mindfulness becomes not just a luxury commodity but a "luxury belief," a status marker that allows the affluent to project virtue while remaining insulated from real-world struggles.
- **Psychological dynamics:** Where the inferiority/superiority complex creates a toxic hierarchy of "enlightened" teachers and perpetual students, often reinforced by misinterpreted neuroscience claims of "superior" meditation brains.
- **Corporate capture:** Where mindfulness in workplaces creates new forms of institutional control and privileged access, making personal development dependent on employment status

and turning corporations into gatekeepers of practice and meaning-making.

- **Institutional control:** Where certification systems function like medieval guilds and standardization stifles genuine adaptation and innovation.
- **Informal power networks:** Where a small inner circle shapes mindfulness's future through unofficial relationships and hidden hierarchies.
- **Knowledge control:** Where wisdom traditions once freely shared become intellectual property, transformed into subscription services and proprietary content, thus creating a troubling cycle where institutions control access in the name of quality while limiting innovation and adaptation.

This chapter strips away the polite pretense to expose how oligarchic structures in mindfulness actively undermine its transformative potential. But more importantly, it lights the way toward a more democratic, accessible, and authentic approach to sharing these practices.

In confronting the reality of power concentration in mindfulness, we're opening the door to genuine transformation. The question isn't whether power structures exist in mindfulness: It's whether we have the courage to dismantle them.

The Anatomy of Oligarchy

Power doesn't always wear a crown. Sometimes it's wrapped in a meditation shawl. In the world of mindfulness and MBSR, oligarchy isn't just possible, it's thriving—often in plain sight. The "rule by the few" that Aristotle described has evolved, shape-shifted, and embedded itself in the very fabric of our spiritual practices. Today's oligarchs don't need titles or treasure chests. They deal in influence. They monopolize knowledge. They shape narratives with a tweet, an app, or a TED Talk.

Sociologist Jaime Kucinskas calls them the "mindful elite." In her 2019 book, *The Mindful Elite: Mobilizing from the Inside Out*, she unravels a paradox: How did a practice rooted in ego dissolution become a breeding ground for new power structures? The answer is both simple and disturbing. Mindfulness didn't spread from the bottom-up. It was a top-down revolution.

A small network of charismatic teachers and researchers strategically positioned mindfulness within prestigious institutions, such as Ivy League universities, Fortune 500 companies, and government agencies. They gave an ancient practice a modern makeover, stripping away its Buddhist roots and recasting it in the language of science and productivity.

It worked. Too well, perhaps.

Now, mindfulness is everywhere. It's also nowhere. It's the air we breathe, invisible but omnipresent. It's the tech guru's app deciding how millions meditate. It's the bestselling author's interpretation of wisdom becoming unquestionable truth. It's the certification board determining who teaches and who remains forever a student.

This new oligarchy doesn't announce itself. It whispers. It speaks the language of celebrity, influence, and money. It convinces us that hierarchy is natural and that some voices matter more than others.

The irony is thick enough to cut with a knife. Mindfulness—a practice rooted in dismantling ego—has become a breeding ground for new power structures:

- "Celebrity teachers" amass followers like Fortune 500 companies.
- Exclusive retreats create a mindfulness aristocracy, where depth of practice is often conflated with depth of pockets.
- Organizations preach non-hierarchy, while a small inner circle makes all the crucial decisions.
- The power to certify teachers rests in the hands of a chosen few, creating gatekeepers of wisdom.

These structures aren't built out of malice. They often arise from genuine desires for quality control or efficiency. But the road to oligarchy is paved with good intentions. Each small concentration of power, each "necessary" hierarchy, lays another brick in the wall—a wall that separates the mindfulness haves from the have-nots.

Kucinskas's research reveals an uncomfortable truth: The very mechanisms that allowed mindfulness to gain widespread acceptance have set the stage for its potential downfall.

The secularization that made mindfulness palatable to the masses has stripped it of its ethical foundations. The institutional adoption that gave it legitimacy has bound it to systems of power and privilege. The network effects that spread the practice have concentrated influence in the hands of a few. We're left with a practice that often looks more like a commodity than a path to liberation, a form of cultural capital where proficiency is a marker of status rather than wisdom.

The Inferiority/Superiority Complex: Mindfulness's Hidden Battle

In the tangled web of human psychology, few threads are as knotted and pervasive as the inferiority/superiority complex. First unraveled by Alfred Adler in the early 20th century (1912), this psychological tug-of-war shapes our lives in ways both subtle and profound. It drives our ambitions, colors our insecurities, and now it's infiltrating the world of mindfulness with alarming consequences.

Adler stumbled upon a universal truth: We all wrestle with feelings of inadequacy. It's our response to these feelings that define us. Some overcompensate, wrapping themselves in a superiority complex like psychological armor. Others remain trapped in self-doubt, their potential suffocated by persistent perceptions of inadequacy.

This dance between feeling "less than" and "better than" becomes the lens through which we view the world, warping our relationships, our goals, and our very sense of self. And nowhere is this dynamic more starkly, or ironically, visible than in the realm of mindfulness.

Witness the absurd paradox: A practice aimed at dissolving the ego becomes the ultimate ego trip. Teachers preaching humility bask in celebrity status as their legions of Instagram followers become a new measure of enlightenment. Students chasing nonattachment compete for validation, turning meditation into a spiritual Olympics. The very tools meant to free us become the bars of a corrupt gilded cage.

This toxic dynamic isn't some new-age novelty. To understand its grip on modern mindfulness, we need to trace its roots back to the Buddhist traditions that shaped the field. These ancient spiritual hierarchies, when filtered through our Western obsession with Eastern wisdom, have created a potent cocktail of superiority that intoxicates both seekers and teachers.

Key ingredients in this toxic brew include:

- Enlightenment as the ultimate prize
- Reincarnated masters born into spiritual royalty
- Blind devotion to infallible gurus
- Theocratic traditions that blur spiritual and worldly power
- Communities that serve the leader, not vice versa
- Western romanticization of all things "Eastern"

Think this is just theoretical hand-wringing? The Shambhala International scandal stands as a chilling reality check. Founded by Chögyam Trungpa, a charismatic teacher who preached "crazy wisdom," Shambhala devolved into a nightmare of unchecked power and rampant abuse.

Trungpa's alcoholism and sexual predation set the stage. His HIV-positive successor knowingly infected followers. The founder's son faced multiple sexual assault allegations as recently as 2018. The community's response? A masterclass in denial: systemic cover-ups, victim-blaming, and a deafening silence that protected abusers at all costs. This wasn't just a failure of individuals, but became a stark revelation of how these hierarchical spiritual systems can rot from within, leaving a trail of shattered lives and betrayed trust.

But wait, there's a new twist in this saga: *neuro-elitism*. Modern science, often filtered through a Tibetan-influenced lens, has inadvertently created a new spiritual aristocracy based on brain scans. Studies show long-term meditators, especially Buddhist monks, have different neural structures. More gray matter here, enhanced connectivity there. Fascinating, sure. But in the hands of the meditation industrial complex and sensationalist media, these findings morph into something far more insidious.

Suddenly, we're not just talking about spiritual advancement. We're talking about "superior" brains. It's a seductive idea that feeds our hunger for quantifiable spiritual progress. The result? A neurological arms race where the size of your hippocampus determines your enlightenment quotient. This perspective isn't just flawed; it's dangerous. If meditation truly created morally superior beings, how do we explain the trail of abuse left by so-called masters? The uncomfortable truth is that even the most seasoned meditators remain painfully human, capable of profound insight and horrific misconduct in equal measure. By putting certain practitioners on a neurological pedestal, we're not just misunderstanding science. We're creating the perfect conditions for unquestioning devotion and a dangerous lack of accountability.

The Siren Song of Enlightened Authority

The allure of oligarchy is seductive. Wouldn't we want the most enlightened minds guiding our practice? Shouldn't those who've spent decades in meditation caves have more say than the novice fumbling with their own breath? This logic is a trap. It's one that countless movements have fallen into. The dangers are real and multifaceted:

- Innovation suffocates when new voices are silenced.
- Echo chambers form, where critical feedback becomes heresy.
- Living wisdom calcifies into dogma, defended by those whose status depends on its immutability.

- The conditions for abuse are created when individuals are elevated to positions of unquestionable spiritual authority.

This inferiority/superiority complex is the hidden current shaping the mindfulness landscape. As we've brought ancient practices into the modern world, we've created a field both ripe with opportunity and fraught with contradiction. Teachers build personal brands while preaching nonattachment. Students chase certifications in pursuit of inner peace. We've woven mindfulness into the fabric of our achievement-oriented society, for better *and* worse.

The challenge lies not in dismantling the mindfulness industry, but in navigating it with clarity and purpose. How do we honor expertise without creating false hierarchies? How do we maintain standards without fostering elitism? These are the koans of our time, puzzles we must solve not in silent retreat, but in the messy reality of building a more mindful field.

Oligarchy's Footprint in Mindfulness and MBSR

The mindfulness world presents a facade of openness, but oligarchy runs deep: a hidden network of power and influence that determines who shapes the future of these practices. Let's rip off the Band-Aid and examine the wounds beneath.

Silence isn't neutral. In the face of oligarchy, inaction isn't just complacency; it's complicity. As we sit idly by, watching the mindfulness world operate through unofficial hierarchies and exclusive relationships, we're not just observers. We're active participants in the erosion of a revolutionary practice.

The Guru Paradox: Authority Versus Empowerment

Mindfulness fosters self-determination, yet we've created a system that elevates certain teachers to near-divine status. It's the guru paradox: We say, "question everything," but don't you dare question the master. This dynamic creates a power imbalance that can distort the entire practice. When we outsource our wisdom to gurus, we're not just deferring to expertise, we're abdicating our own authority. And in that gap, oligarchy thrives. The result? A mindfulness culture where the words of a few carry more weight than the lived experiences of many, where breakthrough insights are attributed to teachers rather than to the practice itself. It's a subtle shift, but a profound one: from empowerment to dependency, from inner exploration to outer validation.

The Hidden Networks: Power Through Connection

Want to see power dynamics in action? Look at how MBSR evolves. As this practice spreads globally, reaching thousands of students through diverse organizations and teachers, a curious pattern emerges. The real influence over its development remains concentrated in informal networks, flowing through personal connections rather than transparent channels.

This creates a fundamental paradox. MBSR needs some consistency to maintain its integrity, but who gets to define that consistency? Currently, significant influence flows through Brown University's Mindfulness Center, not through any official authority, but through unofficial relationships and historical connections. This informal power structure shapes MBSR's development without clear processes for broader input or innovation.

The impact? While thousands of teachers work directly with students worldwide, gathering valuable insights about what works and what doesn't, their voices often go unheard. Experience in the field matters less than connections to the right networks. Innovation struggles to break through, not because it lacks merit, but because it lacks the right relationships.

This isn't a bug in the system. It *is* the system. Want your teaching innovations recognized? Better have the right connections. Want to contribute insights from years of active teaching? Good luck finding official channels for that input. The result is a practice that evolves through whispered conversations rather than open dialogue, maintaining power through subtle exclusion while preaching inclusivity.

The irony cuts deep: A practice meant to cultivate clear seeing has developed blind spots to its own power structures. We've created a system where unofficial influence matters more than documented impact. It's time to bring these hidden networks into the light. The future of MBSR demands more than good intentions; it requires transparent structures that truly empower the entire teaching community.

Mindfulness as a Luxury Belief

As the wealth gap in society reaches historic levels, mindfulness has become another domain where economic inequality shapes access and outcomes. Consider the stark reality: while the richest 1 percent capture an ever-growing share of global wealth, mindfulness programs increasingly price themselves at levels that exclude the majority of people:

- Teacher training programs cost $10,000-plus when median savings accounts hold less than $5,000.
- Multiday retreats are priced at thousands of dollars in an era where 64 percent of Americans live paycheck to paycheck.
- Certification processes often require investments equivalent to a semester of college.
- Ongoing training fees exceed monthly grocery budgets for many families.
- Premium access tiers match typical monthly rent payments.

The timing is particularly cruel. Just as economic stress and mental health challenges surge among working- and middle-class populations, the very practices that could help are becoming increasingly out of reach. This creates a perverse dynamic:

- Those facing the greatest financial stress have the least access to stress-reduction tools.

- Communities hit hardest by economic inequality get priced out of resilience training.
- Working-class people struggling with anxiety can't afford anxiety-management programs.
- Marginalized groups experiencing trauma lack access to trauma-sensitive mindfulness.

The Shift from Luxury Good to Luxury Belief

Beyond cost barriers, mindfulness has undergone a deeper transformation, one that aligns with what psychologist and cultural commentator Rob Henderson calls luxury beliefs. Henderson, who grew up in foster care, served in the US Air Force, and later earned a PhD from Cambridge, developed this concept after observing how elite institutions promote ideas that signal status but impose real burdens on others. In his view, affluent individuals no longer rely on luxury goods like watches, yachts, and private clubs to distinguish themselves. Instead, they use luxury beliefs—status-signaling ideas that cost them little but often create hardship for those without their economic privilege.

Mindfulness increasingly operates in this way. It's no longer just an expensive wellness practice; it has become a cultural marker, a way for affluent individuals to project virtue and self-awareness while remaining insulated from the struggles that make mindfulness unattainable for others.

Consider the gaslighting effect this creates:

- The "right" way to eat: mindfully, with organic, locally sourced ingredients
- The "proper" approach to parenting: conscious, present, unhurried
- The "enlightened" way to work: balanced, purposeful, fulfilling
- The "correct" relationship to time: spacious, unrushed, abundant

These mindfulness-influenced ideals sound wonderful in theory. But they often assume a level of economic privilege that most people simply don't have.

A single parent working two jobs doesn't have the time or resources for "mindful eating" with organic food. A warehouse worker can't demand "purposeful" work when they need to make rent. A gig worker living paycheck to paycheck doesn't have the luxury of an "unrushed" relationship to time.

Yet rather than acknowledging these economic realities, mindfulness culture often frames these limitations as personal failures, a lack of commitment, awareness, or wisdom. The inability to maintain a daily meditation practice is treated as a moral shortcoming rather than an economic constraint. The stress of financial precarity becomes something to "observe with nonjudgment" rather than a real injustice to address.

This is where luxury beliefs impose real burdens. They shift the blame for suffering onto individuals rather than systemic conditions. The mindfulness industry, much like elite institutions, presents stress as a personal issue to "manage" rather than a consequence of larger forces like stagnant wages, corporate exploitation, and the erosion of job security.

A Self-Reinforcing Cycle of Exclusion

The transformation of mindfulness into a luxury belief has created a widening gap between those who can access its benefits and those who cannot. The cycle looks like this:

1. High costs limit access to affluent participants.
2. Programs cater increasingly to wealthy demographics.
3. Teaching emphasis shifts from addressing suffering to optimizing privilege.
4. Marketing focuses on luxury and exclusivity.

5. Prices continue rising as mindfulness becomes a premium product.

6. The wealth gap in mindfulness access grows wider.

This isn't just an economic issue; it's an ideological shift that has reshaped mindfulness at its core. As mindfulness has become more exclusive, it has also become detached from the realities of working-class life.

Mindfulness as a Tool of Social Sorting

The consequences ripple through the entire field:

- Teachers feel pressure to target wealthy clients to sustain their own livelihoods.
- Programs emphasize comfort over transformation to retain affluent customers.
- Cultural elements get sanitized for upper-class tastes.
- Working-class perspectives become increasingly rare in mindfulness spaces.
- The revolutionary potential of mindfulness to address systemic suffering gets dulled.

This is the true danger of mindfulness as a luxury belief: It distorts how we understand suffering itself. By turning economic struggle into an issue of "mindset" rather than material reality, mindfulness culture gaslights those experiencing financial hardship, offering personal insight while ignoring structural inequality.

At precisely the historical moment when mindfulness is most needed to address rising economic anxiety and stress, it has become a marker of the very inequality driving that suffering. Unless we actively work to democratize access, mindfulness risks reinforcing society's divides rather than helping to heal them.

The challenge ahead is not just making mindfulness more affordable; it's ensuring that it remains a practice for all, not just a status symbol for the privileged few.

The Standardization Paradox

The relationship between standardization and mindfulness requires nuanced understanding. Some degree of standardization is necessary; it allows for research validation, ensures basic quality, and makes practices accessible to diverse populations. The problem isn't standardization itself, but rather how it's currently implemented.

Current MBSR standardization serves institutional control:

- Rigid protocols that can't adapt to local needs
- Centralized decision-making about acceptable modifications
- Expensive certification processes controlling who can teach
- One-size-fits-all approaches that ignore cultural contexts
- Standardization used as a tool for brand protection

What we need instead is standardization that serves practitioners:

- Clear core practices with documented principles for adaptation
- Transparent frameworks for maintaining quality while allowing innovation
- Community-driven processes for evaluating modifications
- Built-in flexibility for cultural and contextual adaptation
- Standardization as a foundation for growth rather than a constraint

The difference lies in who controls the standards and how they're implemented. When standardization comes from centralized authority focused on control, it stifles growth. When it emerges from community wisdom focused on empowerment, it enables flourishing while maintaining integrity.

Who Owns Mindfulness?

The commodification of mindfulness presents a stark paradox. Practices that were freely shared for millennia, intended to liberate the mind, have become intellectual property. Ancient wisdom traditions are now packaged products, locked behind paywalls and restricted by copyright. Even MBSR's curriculum and teaching materials remain tightly controlled, accessible only through select institutions despite their origins in freely shared contemplative practices.

This transformation goes beyond simple commercialization. Software companies have turned mindfulness into a subscription service. Luxury retreats market enlightenment at premium prices. Teachers become unwitting gatekeepers, bound by licensing agreements and institutional controls. What began as communal wisdom, passed freely from teacher to student, has become, in some cases, a gated commodity available only to those who can afford it.

The current system creates a troubling cycle. Institutions control access to maintain quality, but these controls concentrate power and limit innovation. MBSR programs, while acknowledging this tension, have attempted to address accessibility issues within the very system that creates them. They offer scholarships and sliding scales, Band-Aids on a structural wound.

What's needed isn't just broader access to existing programs, but a fundamental reimagining of how mindfulness is shared and taught. If these practices are truly meant for collective liberation, we must question not just who owns mindfulness, but whether it should be owned at all. The challenge isn't simply making current programs more accessible; it's creating new models that honor both quality and openness, both depth and availability.

Stifled Innovation and Adaptation in Mindfulness Practices

Oligarchy is the enemy of innovation. When power concentrates in the hands of a few, fresh ideas suffocate. The mindfulness world, once a vibrant ecosystem of diverse practices, risks becoming a monoculture.

Think about it. How many truly new approaches to mindfulness have emerged from within established organizations in the past decade? We're rehashing the same techniques, repackaging ancient wisdom in shiny new wrappers, but where's the genuine evolution?

This stagnation is dangerous. As the world changes at breakneck speed, mindfulness needs to adapt to remain relevant. But adaptation requires experimentation, risk-taking, and a willingness to challenge established norms—all things that oligarchic structures actively discourage.

The cost? A practice that grows increasingly out of touch with the realities of modern life. Techniques that fail to address emerging challenges. A missed opportunity to harness new technologies and insights to deepen our understanding of the mind.

Exclusion and Lack of Diversity in Mindfulness Communities

Oligarchy breeds homogeneity. As access to mindfulness becomes increasingly gated—by money, by connections, by cultural background—we create echo chambers.

Look around at the next mindfulness retreat or MBSR training. Notice anything? The lack of diversity isn't just an optics problem. It's a fundamental limitation on the depth and breadth of the practice itself. When mindfulness communities lack diversity, we miss out on:

- Unique perspectives that could enrich our understanding of the practice

- Cultural wisdom that could deepen our approach to mental well-being
- Lived experiences that could challenge our assumptions and biases

The result is an ethical failure and a practical one. We end up with a narrow, culturally specific version of mindfulness that fails to serve vast swathes of humanity.

Erosion of Mindfulness's Transformative Potential

At its core, mindfulness is revolutionary. It's about seeing through illusions, questioning assumptions, and fundamentally changing our relationship with ourselves and the world. But under the weight of oligarchy, this radical potential gets dulled.

Instead of a tool for profound personal and social transformation, mindfulness risks becoming:

- A Band-Aid for systemic issues
- A way to cope with, rather than change, oppressive conditions
- A practice that reinforces, rather than challenges, existing power structures

The bitter irony? The more successful mindfulness becomes in its watered-down, oligarchy-approved form, the further it drifts from its transformative roots.

The Corporate Challenge: Power and Access

The rise of workplace mindfulness programs presents a complex challenge in the landscape of institutional power. While these programs can genuinely support employee well-being, they risk creating new forms of privilege and control. As sociologist Carolyn Chen documents in *Work Pray Code* (2022), corporations, particularly in tech, haven't just adopted mindfulness practices; they've reshaped them into comprehensive systems of meaning-making and personal development.

This transformation raises crucial questions about power and access:

- Institutional Control
    - Companies become gatekeepers of practice and development.
    - Mindfulness gets reshaped for productivity over transformation.
    - Programs normalize excessive demands rather than challenge them.
    - Personal growth becomes tied to corporate membership.
- Access and Equity
    - Quality mindfulness training becomes a luxury benefit.
    - Practice communities get bounded by organizational walls.
    - Access depends on employer resources and priorities.
    - Career transitions can sever practice support.
- Systemic Implications
    - New hierarchies are created based on employer resources.
    - Independent communities are replaced with corporate ones.
    - Personal development becomes dependent on employment.
    - Career changes put continuity of practice at risk.

The solution involves reimagining the role of workplace programs. This means developing approaches that:

- Keep practices portable across job changes.
- Build independent community structures.
- Ensure access beyond employment.
- Foster autonomous practice skills.
- Create sustainable support systems.

In essence, workplace mindfulness must serve democratization rather than reinforce existing power structures. Success requires frameworks that transcend organizational boundaries, ensuring practices remain accessible regardless of employment status or corporate access.

Reimagining MBSR: A Community-Centric Vision

The mindfulness industry has become a labyrinth of contradictions. It preaches nonattachment while building empires. It talks of universal wisdom while erecting barriers to entry. It champions inner peace while fostering competition among practitioners. It's time to face an uncomfortable truth: The very structures built to spread mindfulness are now strangling its potential.

But revolutions don't start with answers. They start with better questions. What if mindfulness wasn't a product to be sold, but a common idea to be shared? What if our practices evolved as quickly as our understanding of the mind? What if the wisest teacher was the collective intelligence of the community itself?

These questions speak to the foundation of a radical reimagining of MBSR and the wider mindfulness ecosystem. This isn't a gentle course correction. It's a seismic shift in how mindfulness is taught, practiced, and integrated into society.

Dismantling the Guru Paradox

To address the problem of elevating certain teachers to near-divine status, consider this approach:

- De-emphasize the teacher's role: a guide, not a guru.
- Encourage peer-to-peer learning and mentoring.
- Emphasize the practice itself over individual teachers.

- Create platforms for sharing personal insights, giving equal weight to all voices.
- Develop transparency protocols for teacher–student relationships.

This approach reinforces that wisdom doesn't reside in a single exalted brain, fostering a culture of collective growth rather than individual worship.

Democratizing Access to Mindfulness

To combat economic gatekeeping and the luxury-ification of mindfulness:

- Implement sliding scale fees for all MBSR programs.
- Develop free, open-source mindfulness resources and curricula.
- Create community-supported meditation centers.
- Offer scholarships and work-exchange programs for retreats and training.
- Develop shorter, more accessible program formats for those with limited time.

These strategies ensure that mindfulness doesn't become a luxury good, making it accessible to those who might need it most.

Customizable, Culturally Responsive MBSR

To avoid the standardization trap and one-size-fits-all approaches:

- Develop modular MBSR programs that can be customized for different cultures and contexts.
- Create pathways for incorporating diverse cultural wisdom into mindfulness practices.
- Encourage adaptation and innovation in mindfulness techniques.

- Implement community feedback loops to continually refine and evolve practices.

This approach preserves the rich tapestry of mindfulness traditions and allows for practices that truly meet the needs of diverse populations.

Open-Source Mindfulness

To challenge the notion of intellectual property in mindfulness:

- Release MBSR curricula and training materials under some form of Creative Commons licensing.
- Create collaborative platforms for developing and refining meditation techniques.
- Encourage cross-pollination between different mindfulness approaches.
- Develop open standards for mindfulness teacher training and certification.

This strategy turns wisdom into community-owned knowledge rather than a commodity, fostering innovation and preventing the concentration of power through knowledge hoarding.

Building Diverse, Inclusive Mindfulness Communities

To address the lack of diversity and creation of echo chambers:

- Implement outreach programs to underrepresented communities.
- Offer training in cultural competence for all mindfulness teachers.
- Create mentorship programs for teachers from diverse backgrounds.
- Ensure diverse representation in leadership roles and decision-making bodies.

These strategies enrich the practice by incorporating a wide range of perspectives and lived experiences.

Ethical Governance and Transparency

To combat the concentration of power and lack of accountability:

- Implement democratic decision-making processes in mindfulness organizations.
- Advance transparency in stewardship and governance.
- Establish independent ethics boards for oversight.
- Develop clear, publicly available ethical guidelines for teachers and organizations.

These measures create a culture of integrity and shared responsibility, preventing the accumulation of unchecked power.

This approach goes beyond surface-level inclusivity; it harnesses the collective intelligence of the entire mindfulness community to make decisions that are stronger, more relevant, and aligned with practitioners' needs. By implementing these interconnected approaches, we can create a mindfulness ecosystem that is more democratic, adaptable, and true to its core principles. This modernized approach doesn't dilute the practice; it enriches it, making it more relevant and impactful in our complex, rapidly changing world. These changes are a practical necessity for mindfulness to remain relevant and potent. In Open MBSR, we address the oligarchic structures in the mindfulness world, reclaiming its revolutionary potential as a force for personal and collective liberation.

A Call to Action

The mindfulness movement stands at a crossroads. What began as a revolutionary practice has calcified into rigid hierarchies and exclusive clubs. The current system elevates certain teachers to near-divine status while erecting economic barriers that would make a country club blush. The result? A mindfulness culture where the words of a few carry more weight than the lived experiences of many, where breakthrough insights are attributed to gurus rather than to the practice itself.

This is the stark reality that's eroding the transformative potential of mindfulness. Practices rooted in renunciation have turned into luxury goods. The mindfulness movement preaches self-reliance while fostering dependency on guided meditations and celebrity experts. It talks of universal wisdom while standardizing one-size-fits-all approaches that flatten the rich tapestry of mindfulness traditions.

But recognition is the first step toward change. By naming these issues, by dragging them into the light, we create the possibility of a different path, a path where mindfulness remains true to its transformative roots, where it serves as a force for genuine awakening and positive change in the world.

Key Takeaways

- The guru paradox: Mindfulness fosters self-determination yet elevates certain teachers to unquestionable status.

- The inferiority/superiority complex in mindfulness creates harmful hierarchies, reinforced by misinterpreted neuroscience claims about "superior" meditation brains.

- Mindfulness has evolved into a "luxury belief" system that gaslights those experiencing hardship by framing systemic issues as personal failures while allowing the affluent to project virtue.

- Hidden power networks and informal relationships, rather than transparent processes, create bottlenecks that stifle innovation and prevent practices from evolving to meet contemporary needs.

- Corporate adoption of mindfulness has transformed personal development into an employment benefit, creating new forms of institutional control and access inequality.

> - Standardization, while necessary for quality, has become a tool for centralized control rather than a foundation for community-driven growth and adaptation.
> - The commodification of ancient wisdom through intellectual property rights has created artificial scarcity in practices meant to be freely shared.

Reflection Questions

1. How do hidden power networks in mindfulness communities influence who gets to shape these practices, and what alternative structures could create more transparent, democratic development?
2. In what ways does treating mindfulness as a "luxury belief" contribute to gaslighting those facing economic hardship, and how can we reframe these practices to acknowledge systemic barriers?
3. How might corporate mindfulness programs be redesigned to serve democratization rather than reinforce existing power structures?
4. What concrete steps can mindfulness organizations take to make their governance and decision-making processes more transparent and inclusive?
5. How can standardization in mindfulness teaching serve practitioner needs rather than institutional control, while maintaining quality and integrity?

These challenges explored aren't insurmountable. They're invitations to embody the very principles of mindfulness as we work to transform it.

Looking Ahead

Part II dared to critique what isn't working. It examined how Buddhist entanglement compromises secular practice, how one-dimensional thinking strips mindfulness of its power, and how oligarchic structures concentrate power in ways that contradict mindfulness's core insights.

Part III dives into the vision of *Open MBSR*: a reimagining of how mindfulness can be taught, practiced, and stewarded. You'll explore concrete strategies for dismantling oligarchic structures, democratizing access, and reclaiming the revolutionary potential of this transformative practice. The path forward isn't about tearing down all structures, but about creating systems that embody the wisdom we seek to cultivate.

Part III

The Open MBSR Framework

The journey so far has taken you deep into the heart of mindfulness. Part I explored the foundations: what mindfulness really is, how it works, and how MBSR revolutionized its application in the modern world. You also learned about unexpected wisdom from diverse sources, from open-source software to Quaker governance, that light the way forward for mindfulness evolution.

Part II pulled back the curtain on the shadow side of contemporary mindfulness: the Buddhist entanglement that threatens secular integrity, the oligarchic structures that concentrate power, and the one-dimensional thinking that strips practices of their transformative depth.

You now stand at a pivotal moment. Part III shifts focus from identifying the challenges of contemporary mindfulness to creating forward-thinking solutions. Here, the book integrates the lessons learned to build a new path—one that honors tradition by evolving it and addresses the limitations of MBSR by transcending them. This is not about discarding the past, but about reimagining it for a more inclusive and transformative future.

- Chapter 8 lays out the *Open MBSR Manifesto,* a revolutionary framework that maintains integrity while fostering evolution. It's not another set of rigid guidelines, but a living document that embraces complexity and champions transparency.

- Chapter 9 translates theory into practice, offering a practical guide for creating spaces where genuine transformation can flourish.
- Chapter 10 confronts the challenges ahead with clear eyes and bold hearts. It addresses the inevitable resistance to change and charts a path forward. This is an invitation to fundamentally reimagine how to cultivate awareness in the modern world.

Chapter 8

The Open MBSR Manifesto

Mindfulness stands at a crossroads. Like many revolutionary movements that achieve rapid mainstream success, it now faces fundamental challenges that threaten to undermine its transformative potential. The scaffolding that supported its swift ascent appears increasingly unstable. Like a tree whose roots have become entangled with neighboring plants, MBSR's Buddhist origins challenge its secular aspirations. Its governance structure has calcified into rigid hierarchies, concentrating power in the hands of a few. Perhaps most concerning, its approach to the rich complexity of human experience has often been reduced to oversimplified formulas and quick-fix solutions.

Yet within these challenges lies an opportunity for evolution. Open MBSR emerges not as a rejection of what came before, but as a natural next step in mindfulness's journey into the modern world. It's a framework built on transparency, inclusivity, and the willingness to engage with life's inherent and sometimes paradoxical complexity, all with the courage to continuously challenge our shadow.

This manifesto serves not as another set of rigid guidelines, but as a framework for transformation. Through clear outcomes that give direction to our practice, principles that honor both wisdom and shadow while maintaining ethical clarity, and attitudes that embrace paradox rather than deny it, we create space for mindfulness to evolve while maintaining its integrity. Most importantly, we establish mechanisms that distribute power, prevent spiritual bypassing, and ensure accessibility for all. Like jazz emerging from blues, Open MBSR derives from its roots while daring to create something authentically new, something that speaks to the challenges and opportunities of our time.

This framework:

- Maintains secular clarity while honoring contemplative wisdom
- Distributes power while preserving quality
- Embraces complexity while remaining accessible
- Allows adaptation while protecting integrity

The following chapters explore each of these elements in detail, examining how they address the fundamental challenges I've identified while opening new possibilities for practice and teaching. Rather than attempting to perfect mindfulness, I endeavor to create conditions for its continuous evolution and authentic expression.

The Five Outcomes: Where Are We Going?

When we talk about transformation, we need to be clear about our destination. Not because we're fixated on goals, but because clarity of intention helps us navigate the journey. Open MBSR identifies five core outcomes that collectively serve as our North Star, not rigid targets to achieve, but horizons toward which we continuously move.

Cultivating Attitudinal Foundations

First is the cultivation of fundamental attitudes and skills, but with a crucial twist. While traditional MBSR teaches attitudes like nonjudgment, patience, and acceptance, Open MBSR recognizes that these aren't simple states to achieve but dynamic tensions to navigate. We learn to hold the paradox of being accepting while maintaining discernment, of cultivating patience while knowing when to act. This isn't about achieving perfect mindfulness; it's about developing the flexibility to dance with life's inherent contradictions.

Practicing Mindfulness Skills

Second comes the practical foundation, the nuts and bolts of mindfulness practice. Here we go beyond traditional meditation and movement practices to explore a broader range of approaches. But crucially, we maintain secular clarity and evidence-based rigor. Think of it as expanding our toolkit while ensuring each tool is both effective and appropriate for its purpose, while at the same time having standard practices that we can do together and that we can learn, teach, and share.

Understanding Stress and Resilience

Third is a deeper understanding of stress and resilience. Beyond learning relaxation techniques, this involves comprehending how our minds and bodies interact with stress, informed by cutting-edge research in neuroscience and psychology. When we understand the mechanism, we can work with stress more skillfully.

Applying Mindfulness to Daily Life

Fourth is the bridge between practice and daily life, perhaps the most crucial outcome of all. Mindfulness isn't just about what happens on our meditation cushion. It's about bringing awareness, balance, and wisdom into our relationships, our work, and our moment-to-moment decisions. This shows up in everything from how we handle difficult conversations and make important choices to how we balance work demands with personal well-being. This is where the rubber meets the road.

Fostering Intentional Community

Finally, and perhaps most revolutionary, is the fostering of intentional community. Traditional MBSR offers group learning, but Open MBSR goes further, creating lasting networks of support and practice. We build communities that know how to navigate conflict mindfully, support each other's practice, and adapt to serve diverse cultural contexts and needs. This effort goes beyond individual transformation by building sustainable independent communities that nurture ongoing growth and development.

These outcomes aren't just checkboxes to tick. They're interweaving threads that create the fabric of a more aware, balanced, and connected life. They give us direction without becoming rigid goals, provide structure without creating new prisons of expectation.

Most importantly, these outcomes address the shadow elements we've identified in mindfulness practice. They prevent the commercialization of quick-fix solutions by emphasizing deep, sustainable change. They counter power concentration by building strong communities. They embrace complexity rather than offering oversimplified answers.

As we move forward, these outcomes serve as both compass and criterion, guiding our development while helping us evaluate our effectiveness. They give us concrete ways to assess our progress while remaining flexible enough to adapt across different contexts and cultures. They remind us that while the path of mindfulness is ancient, its expression must evolve to meet the challenges of our time.

The Seven Principles: The Guiding Pillars of Open MBSR

In the wild frontier of modern mindfulness, where profit often trumps purpose and guru-worship masquerades as empowerment, we need more than good intentions. We need clear, actionable principles that cut through the fog of commercialized spirituality and stealth Buddhism. These seven principles aren't just noble ideals; they're the backbone of a revolution in how we approach mindfulness practice, teaching, and community building.

Act with Integrity and Transparency

- Explicitly document and share origins, influences, and methods.
- Maintain clear, documented boundaries and ethical guidelines.

- Make governance decision-making processes and rationales visible.

Ground in Scientific Evidence and Reason

- Use secular- and science-based language and explanations.
- Base claims and methods on research and evidence.
- Acknowledge limitations and potential adverse effects.

Engage Critically and Think Dialectically

- Actively engage with individual and collective shadow aspects.
- Hold paradoxes and competing perspectives without forcing resolution.
- Actively seek critical perspectives and guard against groupthink.

Embrace Diversity and Ensure Accessibility

- Reduce economic and cultural barriers.
- Create inclusive spaces welcoming all political backgrounds, religious backgrounds, and cultural backgrounds.
- Provide teaching framework, course materials, and resources freely.

Empower Individuals and Respect Autonomy

- Encourage self-guided silent practice.
- Avoid manipulative practices and guru-like dependent relationships.
- Enable organic grassroots communities of practice.

Learn from Direct Experience and Collective Wisdom
- Investigate and speak from direct personal experience.
- Grow together through communal learning and group practice.
- Encourage innovation while ensuring quality adaptations.

Adapt Continuously and Cultivate Growth
- Establish regular community feedback and review processes.
- Update framework based on new research and community needs.
- Document changes and their rationale transparently.

These principles comprise our compass and our shield. They protect against the shadow of spiritual materialism while illuminating a path forward. Through them, we create a practice that's as rigorous as it is accessible, as adaptable as it is authentic. Going beyond making mindfulness available to all, we transform it into a truly democratic force for individual and collective growth, free from the hidden agendas and power structures that have held it back for too long.

The 9+1 Attitudes: Beyond One-Dimensional Mindfulness

Chapter 2 explored Jon Kabat-Zinn's nine attitudes of mindfulness. They're powerful tools, and potentially dangerous ones. Without proper framing and understanding, they become weapons of spiritual bypassing: "nonjudging" breeds moral paralysis; "acceptance" enables toxic passivity; "letting go" becomes emotional numbness. We've seen these distortions play out across the mindfulness landscape, creating the very suffering these practices aim to address and alleviate.

The solution isn't to reinvent the wheel. Open MBSR adds just one attitude, *dialectical fluidity*, but this addition transforms all the others. Like a catalyst in a chemical reaction, this "+1" attitude fundamentally changes how we understand and practice the original nine. It's not about replacing Kabat-Zinn's framework; it's about evolving it to meet the challenges identified throughout this book.

Drawing from the exploration of dialectical thinking in Chapter 6, I pair each attitude with its complementary opposite. This isn't compromise; it's completion. Like the Taoist concept of yin and yang, each pair forms a dynamic whole greater than its parts. This approach directly addresses the one-dimensional thinking that plagues modern mindfulness, creating space for the full spectrum of human experience.

Let's break down how these attitude pairs work in practice:

- **Nonjudging and critical engagement:** Simple "nonjudging" can become moral paralysis. Instead, we cultivate the ability to pause before reacting while maintaining our capacity for discernment. Picture sitting with a difficult emotion: We observe it without immediate reaction, yet maintain the clarity to recognize when it's signaling something that needs attention. It's the difference between knee-jerk judgment and thoughtful evaluation.

- **Patience and proactive change:** Patience isn't passive waiting. True patience includes knowing when to act. Like a gardener who knows both when to wait for seeds to sprout and when to pull weeds, we learn to distinguish between helpful waiting and harmful passivity. This dynamic approach prevents the trap of toxic acceptance discussed in Chapter 5.

- **Beginner's mind and leveraging experience:** While beginner's mind opens us to fresh possibilities, we'd be fools to ignore hard-won wisdom. Consider a long-term meditator encountering a new practice: They bring both openness to the novel experience and discernment from years of practice. This balance steers us away from both rigid expertise and naive openness.

- **Trust and discernment:** Blind trust is as dangerous as chronic suspicion. Like knowing when to trust your meditation teacher's guidance and when to question their methods, we build the capacity to trust our inner wisdom while maintaining healthy skepticism. This addresses the guru-worship problem exposed in Chapter 7.

- **Non-striving and goal orientation:** Here's a paradox: Effective action often comes from a place of non-striving. Like an archer who must remain relaxed to hit the target, we learn to hold our goals lightly. In meditation, we aim for present-moment awareness precisely by letting go of trying to achieve anything.

- **Acceptance and advocacy for change:** Remember the critique of McMindfulness in Chapter 5? True acceptance isn't resignation. We accept reality precisely so we can change it more effectively. It's like a martial artist who yields to an opponent's force to better redirect it, revolutionary acceptance not passive submission.

- **Letting go and emotional engagement:** Letting go doesn't mean becoming emotionally numb. In group practice, we might fully feel compassion for others' struggles while not getting lost in their stories. This balance prevents the emotional bypassing that plagues many mindfulness programs.

- **Gratitude and acknowledgment of challenges:** Toxic positivity helps no one. When facing illness, we can appreciate our body's resilience while honestly confronting our human limitations. Real gratitude can coexist with clear recognition of life's difficulties.

- **Generosity and boundaries:** The mindfulness world's shadow often shows up in boundary violations disguised as generosity. Like a teacher who shares wisdom freely while maintaining clear professional boundaries, we learn that true generosity includes honoring our own limits.

- **Dialectical fluidity (the +1):** This capstone attitude transforms all others. It's the meta-skill of moving fluidly between seemingly opposite qualities as circumstances require. Think of a skilled mindfulness teacher adapting their approach for different students, firm with one, gentle with another, always responsive to what's needed now.

This dialectical framework is intensely practical. It transforms mindfulness from a set of rigid ideals into a living, breathing practice capable of meeting life's complexity. It's not seeking perfect balance but developing the wisdom to dance between these complementary qualities as situations demand.

Flexibility Through Explicit Framework

This book has explored MBSR's shadow side: a rigid system that preaches flexibility while enforcing conformity through hierarchical control. Meanwhile, McMindfulness proliferates unchecked, creating a troubling paradox, a mindfulness landscape that manages to be simultaneously overcontrolled at its core and dangerously diluted at its edges.

The solution isn't abandoning structure. It's making the implicit explicit. Traditional MBSR operates through unspoken rules, hidden influences, and guru-to-disciple transmission. This opacity creates the perfect conditions for both calcified rigidity and unchecked dilution. When power structures operate in shadows, they resist both scrutiny and evolution.

Drawing from open-source principles, Open MBSR is proposing something radical: complete transparency about what makes mindfulness work. No more stealth Buddhism masquerading as secular practice. No more hidden power structures controlling who can teach and how. No more unwritten rules passed down through whispered lineages. Every element of the framework, from outcomes and principles to attitudes and methods, must be laid bare for examination, discussion, and evolution.

Like the most successful open-source projects, this explicit framework provides both structure and freedom. Consider Linux: rigorous standards for code quality coexist with radical transparency about decision-making and contribution processes. Its strength comes not from restricting access but from documenting exactly how everyone can participate meaningfully while maintaining integrity. By making the implicit explicit in mindfulness practice, we create space for both stability and innovation.

The following sections explain how to implement this transparency across every aspect of mindfulness practice and teaching. They explore specific mechanisms for maintaining quality without creating new hierarchies, for fostering evolution while preserving core benefits, and for building genuine community ownership of these transformative practices.

Breaking Down the Walls While Maintaining Integrity

Remember the discussion of derivation versus recontextualization in Chapter 5? This is where it gets real. An explicit framework lets us:

- Adapt without diluting
- Innovate while maintaining essence
- Evolve without losing our way

Like Agile methodology's shift from rigid processes to flexible frameworks, this creates space for innovation within clear boundaries. But unlike corporate mindfulness's "anything goes" approach, this approach maintains rigor through transparency.

From Program Purity to Framework Integrity

The old model is obsessed with program purity, exact session lengths, precise protocols, and rigid requirements. It's like trying to preserve a language by forbidding it to evolve. Open MBSR proposes something different:

- Focus on outcomes over formats
- Emphasize principles over procedures
- Value adaptation over replication

This approach, inspired by open-source software development, allows for:

- Cultural adaptations that honor rather than appropriate
- Time-flexible formats that maintain effectiveness (If 45 minutes of required daily meditation is not feasible, why not try 20 minutes?)
- Context-sensitive applications that preserve integrity
- Various formats (For example, instead of an 8- or 12-week course, try self-paced options or other approaches.)

Community Oversight Without Oligarchy

Here's where Open MBSR borrows from both open-source governance and Quaker collective wisdom:

- Transparent peer-review processes for innovations
- Distributed decision-making about adaptations
- Collective responsibility for quality maintenance

When a teacher in Seoul adapts the body scan for Korean cultural context, or a facilitator in São Paulo develops a new approach for favela residents, the framework provides clear criteria for evaluation while the community provides collective wisdom for validation.

Addressing the Shadow

This explicit framework tackles the shadow elements identified in this book:

- Prevents stealth Buddhism through complete transparency
- Disrupts power concentration through distributed oversight
- Maintains quality without creating new hierarchies
- Enables innovation while preventing dilution

Practical Implementation

This isn't theoretical. It means:

- Clear documentation of all elements
- Transparent processes for adaptation
- Open channels for community review
- Explicit criteria for evaluation
- Shared repositories of innovations

Like the evolution of algebra from Islamic scholarship discussed earlier, this is creating a universal language for mindfulness practice, one that can cross cultures while maintaining integrity.

This is mindfulness growing up, shedding both the rigidity of traditionalism and the "anything goes" approach of McMindfulness. It's a framework as robust as it is flexible, as clear as it is adaptable.

A Note on Evidence and Research

The revolution in mindfulness practice I am proposing must be grounded in evidence, not just intention. While Open MBSR incorporates practices with robust scientific validation, this new framework demands its own systematic study and verification. The core practices—body scan, mindful movement, and awareness of breath—carry decades of research support. However, their function within Open MBSR's unique structure requires fresh examination.

A critical issue in current MBSR research demands attention: MBSR teachers receive certification through various institutions, each with their own curriculum and standards for teaching. While all these institutions trace back to the original UMass Medical Center program, they have evolved different approaches, with some organizations developing their own certification processes and training methods. This diversity in teacher training, combined with varying interpretations of the curriculum, has led to significant differences in how MBSR is actually taught. While this organic evolution has allowed MBSR to spread, it makes standardized research evaluation challenging. These variations, rarely documented in research, make it difficult to determine which elements drive outcomes or to make meaningful comparisons between studies.

Open MBSR addresses this challenge through a paradoxical innovation: By explicitly defining its core principles, practices, and outcomes with greater precision than traditional MBSR, it actually enables more consistent implementation even while allowing for structured variation. The Open MBSR Manifesto provides clear guidelines about what elements must remain constant, from the foundational practices to the teaching principles to the intended outcomes. This strong foundation allows you to systematically study variations in format, such as "Open MBSR 12-week/1.5-hour sessions/20-minute daily practice" or "Open MBSR 8-week/2.5-hour sessions/45-minute daily practice." Because the essential elements are well-defined, you can better evaluate how different formats influence results while maintaining program integrity.

While traditional MBSR's risks and benefits have been documented through decades of research, I must be explicitly clear: Open MBSR's unique approach may present different challenges and opportunities that we have yet to discover. This uncertainty is not a weakness but an opportunity for honest investigation. As we implement this framework, we commit to transparent documentation of both positive and adverse effects, acknowledging that our understanding will evolve through systematic observation and research.

This commitment to rigorous evaluation includes:

- Systematic documentation of both benefits and adverse effects across diverse contexts
- Regular assessment of teaching methods and their impacts on practitioner development

- Clear protocols for identifying, addressing, and reporting difficulties as they emerge
- Transparent sharing of findings—both positive and challenging—with the broader mindfulness community
- Detailed documentation of program variations and their specific impacts
- Ongoing monitoring for unexpected or novel risks that may emerge

The research agenda prioritizes:

- Comparative studies examining effectiveness across different Open MBSR formats
- Impact analysis of varying session lengths and practice requirements
- Benefits and challenges of different teaching progressions
- Long-term effects on practice sustainability across program variations
- Cultural adaptations and their differential outcomes
- Systematic evaluation of which program elements drive specific outcomes

This goes beyond validating a new approach. It's about creating a framework where transparency and uncertainty can coexist with rigorous methodology. By establishing clear categories for program variations while maintaining core principles, Open MBSR enables both flexibility and meaningful research comparison. We invite the broader mindfulness research community to join us in rigorously examining these methods and testing our framework's premises, including careful attention to both benefits and potential risks as they emerge.

A Framework for Revolution

The Open MBSR Manifesto isn't just another set of guidelines for teaching mindfulness. It's a declaration of independence from the forces that have constrained mindfulness's potential. In a world where McMindfulness peddles quick fixes and spiritual materialism masquerades as transformation, the Open MBSR Manifesto outlines something radically different.

A framework built on four pillars:

- Outcomes that give clear direction without creating new prisons of expectation
- Principles that ensure integrity without fostering rigidity
- Attitudes that embrace complexity rather than enforce toxic positivity
- Flexibility that allows evolution while maintaining potency

But manifestos are worthless without action. This framework demands more than intellectual agreement; it requires a personal commitment, a teaching revolution, and a community transformation.

Personal Commitment

- Embracing complexity in your own practice
- Engaging critically with traditional approaches
- Working actively with shadow elements
- Building genuine independence

Teaching Revolution

- Dismantling guru dynamics
- Fostering student autonomy
- Embracing dialectical approaches
- Maintaining ethical clarity

Community Transformation

- Distributing power rather than concentrating it
- Creating inclusive, accessible spaces
- Fostering genuine dialogue and debate
- Supporting collective evolution

The goal is to liberate mindfulness. The question isn't whether mindfulness will evolve, but whether that evolution will lead to deeper commercialization or genuine transformation.

As you move into the practical applications in the next chapter, remember that this framework isn't a destination but a launch pad. Its power lies not in perfect implementation but in the revolutionary spirit it embodies. Each element, outcomes, principles, attitudes, and flexibility, creates space for mindfulness to breathe, grow, and truly serve human flourishing.

Key Takeaways

- The five core outcomes of Open MBSR provide direction without rigidity:
  - Cultivating attitudinal foundations
  - Practicing mindfulness skills
  - Understanding stress and resilience
  - Applying mindfulness to daily life
  - Fostering intentional community
- The seven guiding principles form the backbone of Open MBSR:
  - Act with integrity and transparency.
  - Ground in scientific evidence and reason.

- Engage critically and think dialectically.
- Embrace diversity and ensure accessibility.
- Empower individuals and respect autonomy.
- Learn from direct experience and collective wisdom.
- Adapt continuously and cultivate growth.

- The 9+1 attitudes transform traditional mindfulness by embracing dialectical thinking, pairing each attitude with its complement to create a more nuanced and complete practice (e.g., nonjudging with critical engagement, acceptance with advocacy for change).

- Making the implicit explicit through clear documentation and transparent processes helps prevent both rigid conformity and unchecked dilution of mindfulness practices.

- Success requires commitment at multiple levels:
  - Personal practice that embraces complexity
  - Teaching that dismantles guru dynamics
  - Community building that distributes rather than concentrates power

Reflection Questions

1. How will you embody these principles in your own practice and teaching?
2. Where do you see opportunities for immediate change?
3. What challenges might arise, and how will you navigate them?
4. How can your local community engage with this framework?

Looking Ahead

The path ahead isn't easy. It demands courage to challenge established norms, wisdom to navigate complexity, and compassion to hold space for transformation. But the potential payoff—a mindfulness practice that's truly accessible, adaptable, and transformative—makes the journey worth every step.

The revolution in mindfulness isn't just possible, it's inevitable. The only question is: Will you help shape it, or watch from the sidelines as others forge the path ahead? The next chapter provides the practical tools to turn this vision into reality. Let's begin.

Chapter 9

Open MBSR Teaching Essentials

The moment of truth has arrived. The book has dissected the problems of modern mindfulness, explored revolutionary solutions, and outlined a bold new vision. Now comes the real test: transforming theory into practice. Think of this chapter as a radical yet practical new teaching manual for liberation through Open MBSR.

The challenge before us is monumental. How do we create teaching guidelines that:

- Maintain rigor without creating new hierarchies?
- Ensure quality without stifling innovation?
- Honor tradition while embracing evolution?
- Build independence rather than dependency?

This chapter bridges the gap between vision and reality, offering a framework that embodies everything explored throughout this book. I am not here to provide another rigid manual or set of unchangeable rules. That would contradict everything I have argued for. Instead, I am offering a living framework that maintains integrity while allowing for evolution and adaptation. We'll return to the earlier jazz analogy because it perfectly captures the essence of this approach. Like jazz musicians, we need to work with fundamental principles and structures while maintaining the freedom to improvise and innovate. Just as jazz isn't bound by the rigid sheet music of classical compositions, this approach allows for creative interpretation within established guidelines. This system operates through three interconnected elements:

- Essential teacher guidance
- Core practices that maintain effectiveness while embracing inclusivity
- A flexible eight-week curriculum that honors consistency and innovation

Let's translate this theoretical framework into practical action. More than a matter of teaching differently, the goal is to fundamentally reimagine the teacher–student relationship in mindfulness.

Essential Teacher Guidance

Let's start by dismantling the guru pedestal. Teaching mindfulness isn't about becoming an enlightened master dispensing wisdom from on high. It's about creating conditions for collective exploration and growth. This section outlines a radically different approach to facilitation: one that distributes power, acknowledges shadow, and maintains ethical integrity while fostering genuine transformation.

Elements Carried Forward

Not everything needs reinvention. Traditional MBSR got some things right, and it's wise to retain them:

- **Experiential learning:** The direct experience of practice remains our primary teacher. No amount of theoretical understanding can replace the wisdom gained through personal exploration.
- **Core practices:** The fundamental toolset—body scan, awareness of breath, mindful movement, walking meditation, open awareness—has proven its worth. While these practices have

roots in contemplative traditions, Open MBSR presents them in a clear secular framework while acknowledging their origins.
- **Daily practice integration:** Regular engagement remains crucial. Transformation doesn't happen through intellectual understanding alone.
- **Group learning:** The power of collective practice and shared exploration continues to be a cornerstone of this approach.
- **Teacher embodiment:** Personal practice still matters. You can't guide others where you haven't gone yourself.

Distinct Elements of Open MBSR

While much of MBSR's core structure remains valuable, Open MBSR introduces key innovations that address the challenges identified throughout this book. These distinct elements aren't just modifications; they're fundamental shifts that transform how mindfulness is taught, practiced, and evolved.

Dialectical Framework

- Embrace paradox and complexity rather than seeking simplistic solutions.
- Balance seemingly opposing elements (acceptance/change, individual/collective, structure/flexibility).
- Encourage critical engagement with practices and concepts.
- Move beyond one-dimensional interpretations of mindfulness.

Distributed Power Structure

- Shift from hierarchical teacher–student dynamics to collaborative learning.
- Implement transparent governance and decision-making processes.

- Create clear ethical guidelines and accountability mechanisms.
- Ensure financial accessibility without creating new hierarchies.

Secular Clarity

- Explicitly acknowledge Buddhist origins while maintaining secular integrity.
- Develop independent, evidence-based frameworks and terminology.
- Avoid stealth Buddhism and spiritual bypassing.
- Create clear boundaries between religious and secular practice.

Adaptable Framework

- Document and share modifications transparently.
- Establish clear criteria for maintaining integrity while allowing innovation.
- Enable cultural and contextual adaptations.
- Build mechanisms for community feedback and evolution.

Shadow Integration

- Actively engage with individual and collective shadow aspects.
- Address power dynamics explicitly.
- Create space for working with difficulty and complexity.
- Maintain critical awareness of blind spots and limitations.

Community Stewardship

- Shift ownership from institutions to practitioner community.
- Create mechanisms for collective evolution and quality maintenance.
- Enable peer-to-peer learning networks and resource sharing.
- Ensure program sustainability without centralized control.

Embracing the Unknown: The Living Practice

After outlining these distinct elements of Open MBSR, you might expect a neat, complete blueprint. But that would contradict everything we've explored. Whether you're teaching, practicing, or simply curious about mindfulness, what matters is how these elements come alive in real-world contexts and communities.

What does dialectical thinking look like when facing personal trauma or supporting others through theirs? How do we maintain clarity about mindfulness's secular nature while honoring its roots? When should we hold firm to structure and when should we adapt? These aren't abstract questions; they're practical challenges that shape how Open MBSR will evolve and serve diverse needs.

This uncertainty isn't a weakness; it's a strength. It prevents the entrenchment of new dogmas, keeps us honest about the complexity of human experience, and creates space for genuine innovation. The practices and curriculum that follow aren't commandments carved in stone. They're starting points for exploration, tools to be adapted thoughtfully through the lens of these distinct elements.

Practices and Exercises

Think of exercises as musical études, focused pieces designed to develop specific skills. An exercise might explore how you perceive stress through reflective journaling or investigate your communication patterns through structured dialogue. These are time-bound activities with clear start and end points, like practicing a particular musical sequence or technique that helps one master a challenging passage in a song.

In contrast, practices are the daily scales and chord progressions of mindfulness, fundamental patterns you return to again and again, each repetition building depth and understanding. The body scan isn't something you do once and check off your list. Neither is following your breath or moving mindfully. These are the basic forms that, through devoted repetition, become the foundation of mastery. They're what transforms mindfulness from a neat idea into a lived reality.

This distinction matters because it affects how we approach each activity. Exercises invite focused exploration, like learning a new musical phrase. Practices demand commitment to the fundamentals, returning daily to the same basic forms until they become second nature. Both matter. Both serve essential functions. But confusing one for the other is like mistaking knowing a single song for mastering an instrument.

Tenets Underlying Core Practices

Every Open MBSR practice embodies five fundamental principles that honor transparency, autonomy, and genuine transformation:

- **Clear Naming**
  - Names practices for what they do, not what they aim to produce
  - Uses straightforward, secular language
  - Avoids promising specific outcomes
  - Enables informed choice
- **Ethical Boundaries**
  - Rejects visualization and guided imagery
  - Prevents emotional manipulation
  - Maintains appropriate teacher–student relationship
  - Respects participant autonomy
- **Clear Instruction**
  - Provides practical, precise guidance
  - Avoids poetic or performative language
  - Focuses on technique rather than experience
  - Uses language that can be replicated by participants
- **Participant Empowerment**
  - Teaches meditation skills rather than leading guided sessions

- Builds confidence in self-guided practice
- Encourages critical thinking and personal agency
- Supports genuine exploration without dependency
- **Progressive Independence**
  - Gradually reduces verbal guidance
  - Increases periods of silence over time
  - Develops self-guidance capacity
  - Leads to fully independent practice

The goal is clear: to create or develop practitioners who can confidently navigate their own meditation practice in silence without external guidance. This serves the broader commitment to transparency, ethical teaching, and genuine transformation.

These Tenets protect against common pitfalls in mindfulness teaching:

- Teacher performance and spiritual bypassing
- Manipulation through visualization or emotional guidance
- Dependency on external instruction
- Power imbalances in the teacher–student relationship

By adhering to these principles, Open MBSR maintains its integrity while fostering genuine, independent practice.

Core Practices

The revolution I am proposing isn't about throwing everything out and starting from scratch. That would be as foolish as a jazz musician refusing to learn scales. Some practices have proven their worth over decades of application and research. Like well-worn tools in a master craftsperson's workshop, they're too valuable to discard. But that doesn't mean we can't refine how we use them. As you'll learn, most practices from MBSR are being adapted for Open MBSR with little to no change. Open MBSR keeps what is effective and proven from MBSR while addressing its shortcomings.

Body Scan

This isn't just a relaxation technique; it's a systematic exploration of your physical reality. Moving attention through the body, you're developing the fundamental skill of noticing what's actually here, not what you think should be here. It's like learning to read the body's native language without trying to edit the story.

Awareness of Breath

The breath isn't special because it's spiritual; it's special because it's always with you. While the most current MBSR curriculum replaced this practice with one called focused attention (where the breath can be substituted with sound and body sensation), Open MBSR reverts this change and maintains breath awareness as the primary approach. It aligns with Buddhist tradition and scientific evidence, whereas the focused attention practice does not.

Mindful Movement

Mindful movement in Open MBSR remains similar to MBSR's approach, maintaining awareness of body movement while exploring capabilities and limitations. Everybody is suitable for this practice, which focuses on moving with awareness rather than achieving perfect form.

Walking Meditation

Walking meditation in Open MBSR follows MBSR's approach, a practice of presence in motion. Movement is movement, regardless of form, whether walking, using a wheelchair, or adapting to different mobility needs.

Open Awareness

Open awareness, sometimes mistakenly referred to as "choiceless awareness," is a practice of expansive and nonjudgmental observation. Imagine it as removing the blinders of focused attention and allowing your awareness to flow naturally, without being confined by habitual patterns or specific points of focus. This approach invites you to be present with the full spectrum of your experience, thoughts, sensations, emotions, and external stimuli, without clinging to or resisting any of them.

These foundational practices remain largely unchanged from MBSR, with the key exception of reverting focused attention back to awareness of breath. This preserves the scientifically validated practices derived from Buddhist tradition while maintaining their core essence and accessibility.

Modified and New Practices

These practices are named for what they do, not what they aim to produce. Each supports direct experience rather than guided imagery or emotional manipulation.

- **Expansive well-wishing (former MBSR programs called this "loving-kindness meditation"):** This isn't about generating feelings or following prescribed phrases. You're simply extending well-wishes outward in expanding circles, using your own words and moving at your own pace. Unlike some "loving-kindness" practices, there's no visualization, no forced emotion, no formulaic phrases. It's about the straightforward act of wishing well, however that naturally arises for you.
- **Stability and adaptability reflection (former MBSR programs used "mountain/lake meditation"):** Unlike its predecessor in MBSR, this isn't a visualization meditation on mountains or lakes. In Open MBSR we don't do visualizations

and this practice therefore needs to be adapted. In Open MBSR it's a direct reflection on stability and adaptability in your life. When do you feel grounded? What helps you stay flexible? No metaphors needed, no imagery required. You're exploring these qualities as they actually show up in your experience, not as poetic ideals.

Born from Open MBSR's commitment to embracing complexity, this practice explores life's natural tensions. You're not trying to resolve opposites or achieve balance. Instead, you're noticing how apparently contradictory qualities already dance together in your experience. It's practical exploration, not philosophical contemplation.

Each practice strips away the cultural, religious, and performative elements that often creep into mindfulness teaching. What's left is clear, direct engagement with your own experience. No special states to achieve. No experiences to manufacture. Just honest exploration of what's already here.

Like scales for a musician or drills for an athlete, these practices build fundamental skills through straightforward repetition. The teacher's role is simple: clear instruction that progressively reduces, supporting your journey toward independent practice.

Practices and Exercises for Life Integration

Beyond formal meditation, these tools bridge practice with daily life. Each serves a specific purpose, teaching clear skills through direct experience.

Integrated Practices

- **STOP practice (from MBSR):** A brief pause in your day. Not another relaxation technique, but a moment to notice where you are, what you're doing, and what options you have. Think of it as your reset button, available anytime.

Mindful eating (from MBSR): Using the everyday act of eating to understand how awareness works. The food is just your teacher, showing you the difference between automatic pilot and present-moment engagement.

Investigative Exercises

Nine dots exercise (from MBSR): A practical lesson in how we box ourselves in with assumptions. Not just a puzzle to solve, but a concrete demonstration of how mental habits limit our perception.

Stress reaction cycle exploration (from MBSR): Understanding your personal stress mechanics. You're mapping your own responses, seeing clearly how stress plays out in your body and mind. No prescribed solutions, just clear seeing.

Self-Reflection Exercises

Communication exercises (from MBSR): Bringing awareness into conversation. It's about noticing what actually happens when you speak and listen, real-time exploration of how you relate with others.

Difficult communications calendar (from MBSR): A systematic investigation of challenging interactions. You're tracking patterns, noticing triggers, and seeing your habitual responses. It's research, and you're both scientist and subject.

Pleasant and unpleasant events calendar (from MBSR): Studying how you relate to what happens, noticing the patterns in what you're drawn to and what you push away. This involves direct observation of your mind's habits.

Midway feedback exercise (from MBSR): A structured opportunity to assess your practice journey halfway through. This reflection helps identify what's working and what needs adjustment, and deepens your understanding of the learning process.

Six-month letter (from MBSR): Writing a letter to your future self during the course, to be opened six months later. This exercise bridges the intensive training period with long-term practice integration.

Think of these practices and exercises as laboratory equipment for studying your own experience. Each reveals something specific about how your mind works, building skills you can use long after the course ends. The teacher's role is to explain the tools clearly, then step back as you learn to use them yourself.

The Role of Inquiry in Open MBSR

Inquiry, the skillful exploration of participants' direct experiences through questioning, represents a crucial element of mindfulness teaching. While MBSR established valuable foundations for this practice, Open MBSR evolves these principles to address the power dynamics and shadow elements identified throughout this book. This section outlines clear frameworks that protect and strengthen inquiry's core purpose: supporting genuine investigation rather than guiding toward predetermined insights.

Core Principles and Guidelines

Traditional MBSR established these essential principles of inquiry:

- Supporting direct investigation of experience rather than theoretical understanding
- Building self-reflection capacity rather than reliance on teacher insight
- Creating conditions for collective learning without establishing teacher authority

Open MBSR reinforces these principles through clear guidelines:

- Maintain focus on immediate, direct experience.
- Use neutral language that doesn't suggest "right" experiences.
- Avoid interpreting or analyzing experiences.
- Support development of investigative skills.
- Create space for multiple perspectives and contradictions.
- Guard against subtle manipulation toward predetermined insights.

These guidelines directly address the challenges of guru dynamics and power concentration identified in Chapter 7. By making the implicit explicit, you create safeguards against the shadow elements that can emerge in teacher–student relationships.

Inquiry in Practice: An Example

Consider this exchange after a body scan practice:

> *Teacher:* "Would someone be willing to share what they noticed?"
>
> *Participant:* "My mind kept wandering to my to-do list. I'm not very good at this."
>
> *Teacher:* "Could you tell me more about what you actually experienced when you noticed your mind wandering?"
>
> *Participant:* "Well, I'd be following the instructions about focusing on my feet, and then suddenly I'd realize I was thinking about tomorrow's meeting."
>
> *Teacher:* "And in that moment of realizing, what was that like?"
>
> *Participant:* "Oh, interesting. There was this clear moment of recognition. Like waking up."

This exchange demonstrates key inquiry principles: staying with direct experience, moving from general statements to specific moments, and supporting discovery without leading. Note how the teacher maintains focus on direct experience while avoiding both validation and correction.

Common Pitfalls

Even experienced teachers can unconsciously slip into responses that create dependency:

- **Therapeutic interpretation:** "It sounds like you're being hard on yourself."
- **Spiritual teaching:** "When you let go of suffering, you can reach Nirvana."
- **Problem solving:** "Try labeling your thoughts as 'thinking.'"
- **Validation seeking:** "Isn't it wonderful how mindfulness helps us?"
- **Leading questions:** "Did you notice how peaceful it felt?"

These pitfalls often emerge from good intentions but can reinforce unhealthy power dynamics and create dependency on teacher validation.

The Teacher's Role

What teachers don't do:

- Validate experiences as "correct"
- Guide toward particular feelings or states
- Solve or fix others' problems
- Position themselves as spiritual authorities

What teachers do:

- Create a safe space for investigation.
- Support precise observation.
- Model genuine curiosity.
- Maintain focus on direct experience.

Beyond Traditional Forms

Open MBSR recognizes that traditional teacher-led inquiry isn't the only valid form. Alternative approaches include:

- Self-reflection practices
- Peer-based inquiry exercises
- Small group investigations
- Written reflection protocols

The principles remain constant, but the methods can adapt to different contexts and needs. This flexibility aligns with Open MBSR's commitment to accessibility and innovation while maintaining practice integrity.

The goal of inquiry is to cultivate a direct and open investigation of experience. By making these principles explicit and offering multiple approaches, you can create more accessible and empowering pathways for genuine exploration while being flexible to serving different communities in various formats.

The Eight-Week Curriculum

The Open MBSR curriculum builds upon the foundation laid by traditional MBSR while incorporating key modifications to align with the principles of inclusivity, transparency, and critical engagement. This curriculum maintains the core structure as well as many of the essential practices of MBSR, recognizing their proven effectiveness. However, it introduces several significant changes.

Major modifications:

- Increased emphasis on secular, evidence-based approaches
- Integration of dialectical thinking and cognitive flexibility
- Introduction of new practices like the Dialectical Reflection Practice
- More explicit focus on teaching how to meditate without guidance in silence
- Encouragement of critical engagement with mindfulness concepts
- Greater flexibility in practice options to accommodate diverse needs
- Enhanced focus on community-driven learning and peer-to-peer exchange

Elements retained from MBSR:

- Core mindfulness practices (body scan, sitting meditation, mindful movement)
- Progressive structure over eight weeks
- All-day practice intensive
- Emphasis on daily practice
- Focus on stress reduction and cultivating present-moment awareness

Eight-Week Open MBSR Curriculum Overview

Orientation session:

- Introduction to Open MBSR: philosophy, structure, and expectations
- Overview of scientific basis for mindfulness practices

- Exploration of participant goals and intentions
- Introduction to core outcomes and Nine Attitudes of Mindfulness
- Brief experiential practice

Week 1: Introduction to Open MBSR

- **Theme:** Cultivating awareness and curiosity
- **Practices:** Body scan, mindful eating, awareness of breath
- Introduction to principles of Open MBSR, emphasizing inclusivity and critical engagement
- Exploration of nonjudging and beginner's mind attitudes

Week 2: Perception and Flexible Thinking

- **Theme:** Exploring multiple perspectives
- **Practices:** Body scan, sitting meditation, introduction to mindful movement
- Introduction to dialectical thinking and cognitive flexibility
- Exploration of patience and trust attitudes

Week 3: Embodied Awareness

- **Theme:** The body as a source of wisdom
- **Practices:** Sitting meditation (breath, body sensations), mindful movement, walking meditation
- Emphasis on inclusive body awareness and trauma-sensitive approaches
- Exploration of non-striving and acceptance attitudes

Week 4: Understanding Stress and Resilience

- **Theme:** Recognizing patterns and cultivating responsiveness
- **Practices:** Sitting meditation (breath, body, sounds, thoughts), mindful movement

- Introduction to Dialectical Reflection Practice
- Exploration of letting go attitude

Week 5: Working with Thoughts and Emotions

- **Theme:** Allowing and investigating experience
- **Practices:** Open awareness meditation, mindful movement, Dialectical Reflection Practice
- Exploring balance between acceptance and change
- Exploration of gratitude and generosity attitudes

Week 6: Mindful Communication and Relationships

- **Theme:** Bringing awareness to interpersonal dynamics
- **Practices:** Sitting meditation, mindful movement, Expansive Well-Wishing practice
- Exploration of mindful listening, speaking, and role of empathy

All-Day Practice Intensive (Between Weeks 6 and 7)

- Extended period of mindfulness practice (7–8 hours)
- Incorporation of various Open MBSR practices, including periods of silence and reflective exercises

Week 7: Mindfulness in Daily Life

- **Theme:** Integrating mindfulness into everyday activities
- **Practices:** Sitting meditation, mindful movement, Stability and Adaptability Reflection
- Reflection on values, lifestyle choices, and practical applications of mindfulness

Week 8: Sustaining Practice and Moving Forward

- **Theme:** Cultivating a personal mindfulness practice
- **Practices:** Body scan, sitting meditation, mindful movement

- Comprehensive review of Nine Attitudes of Mindfulness with dialectical approach
- Review of key learnings, discussion of ongoing resources, and community support

While this curriculum provides a standard eight-week structure, Open MBSR recognizes the need for flexibility to meet diverse community needs. As Open MBSR evolves, these lessons may be delivered in various formats, durations, or sequences. The challenge moving forward will be to find the right balance between maintaining the integrity and effectiveness of the program while allowing for adaptability to different contexts and populations. This flexibility is a key aspect of Open MBSR's commitment to inclusivity and accessibility.

Progressive Independence: From Guidance to Silence

The development of genuine independence lies at the heart of Open MBSR. While the modern mindfulness industry often creates dependency through constant guidance, this approach systematically develops practitioners' capacity for silent, self-directed practice. Here's the week-by-week progression.

Weeks 1–2: Foundation Building

- Clear, detailed instruction
- Explanation of progression toward silence
- Introduction to basic self-guidance techniques

Weeks 3–4: Growing Independence

- Reduced guidance with longer silent periods
- Tools for working with difficulty independently
- Practice periods alternating between guided and silent segments

Weeks 5–6: Deepening Silence

- Minimal instruction, predominantly silent practice
- Focus on building confidence in self-guidance
- Group discussions about experiences with silence

Weeks 7–8: True Independence

- Brief opening cues leading to extended silence
- Emphasis on trust in direct experience
- Support for establishing independent practice routines

Supporting the Transition

- Addressing common challenges proactively
- Providing clear frameworks for self-guidance
- Creating safe spaces to discuss difficulties
- Offering specific techniques for working with resistance

Benefits of Silent Practice

- Strengthens genuine concentration through direct engagement with distractions
- Builds confidence in one's innate capacity for awareness
- Allows for authentic discoveries unbounded by others' words
- Develops true resilience through unmediated experience

This progression is about revealing the true potential of meditation. Like removing training wheels from a bicycle, the transition might feel difficult and uncertain at first, but it opens the door to genuine freedom and mastery.

The goal isn't to eliminate guidance entirely in the training process but to place it in its proper context: as a temporary support rather than a permanent necessity. Through this careful progression, practitioners discover their own capacity for presence and insight, free from dependency on external voices.

Flexibility Without Compromise

While the sequence can adapt to different contexts, these elements are nonnegotiable:

- No visualization, guided imagery, or emotional manipulation
- Progressive reduction in teacher guidance
- Increasing periods of silence
- Focus on independent practice skills

This framework isn't about preserving tradition. It's about systematically building the skills for genuine, independent mindfulness practice.

The Work Begins Now

I have now laid out the practical blueprint for Open MBSR, but this is just the beginning. The real work happens not in these pages, but in meditation halls, community centers, and wherever people gather to practice mindfulness. The framework I've outlined provides structure without constraint, guidance without rigidity.

To support this work, my organization *Mindful Leader* will be releasing additional free resources, including:

- The Open MBSR Teacher Curriculum Guide
- A free Open MBSR introductory training program
- Additional teaching materials and practice resources

This section represents only the initial foundation. More open-source resources and materials will be made freely available as we continue developing and refining the Open MBSR framework together.

Rather than the traditional chapter takeaways, this chapter focuses on the practical principles that will guide implementation.

> **Key Takeaways**
>
> - Start where you are with what you have.
> - Adapt thoughtfully while maintaining integrity.
> - Document and share your innovations.
> - Learn from challenges and setbacks.
> - Stay connected to the broader Open MBSR community.

Reflection Questions

1. How can we maintain quality while fostering innovation?
2. What metrics tell us we're succeeding?
3. How do we ensure these practices remain truly accessible?
4. When should we hold firm to structure and when should we adapt?

Looking Ahead

This framework isn't a final destination but a starting point for evolution. Like the practices themselves, it will grow and change through engaged application. Your experiences, challenges, and innovations will help shape its future.

The revolution in mindfulness teaching begins now, not with grand gestures but with small, intentional shifts in how we approach each moment of instruction. Every time you step back instead of stepping in, every silence you allow to deepen, every student you empower rather than instruct: These are the building blocks of transformation.

As you move forward with these tools, stay connected to the core principles that brought us here: transparency, empowerment, and genuine transformation. The future of mindfulness teaching isn't set in stone; it's being shaped by each of us, one practice at a time.

The question now isn't whether this approach will work. It's whether we are willing to embrace a way of teaching that systematically dismantles our own authority while building true independence in our students. The path is clear. The tools are in your hands. The revolution in mindfulness teaching begins with you.

Chapter 10

Charting the Path Forward

The moment has arrived to move from theory to practice. This book has exposed fundamental issues in modern mindfulness: from Buddhist entanglement and oligarchic control to one-dimensional thinking. It has outlined a revolutionary framework through Open MBSR. But frameworks alone don't create change. This final chapter focuses on the practical work of implementation.

Three critical tasks lie ahead:

- Addressing legitimate concerns about this transition
- Establishing clear practices at every level, from individual practice to institutional structures
- Creating robust protections to maintain integrity as we grow

This isn't just another program or set of techniques. It's a fundamental reimagining of how mindfulness can serve humanity in our rapidly evolving world. The framework exists. The practices are tested. The community is forming. What happens next depends on how we—as teachers, students, practitioners, and communities—bring these principles to life.

Addressing Common Objections

Before outlining the path forward, this section addresses some important questions and concerns you may have. Not only do these understandable objections deserve attention; they also help clarify why Open MBSR is necessary and how it builds upon rather than diminishes what came before.

"I took MBSR and it transformed my life. Why fix what isn't broken?"

This is perhaps the most heartfelt objection, and it comes from a place of genuine gratitude and experience. If MBSR transformed your life, that's wonderful, and nothing about Open MBSR diminishes that transformation. But personal benefit, however profound, doesn't negate systemic issues. We can simultaneously honor the life-changing impact MBSR has had for many while acknowledging its structural limitations and working to make its benefits more widely accessible.

"What about the extensive research validating MBSR's effectiveness?"

The research supporting MBSR's effectiveness is indeed substantial and valuable. Open MBSR builds upon this foundation rather than dismissing it. The core practices that research has validated—mindful movement, awareness of breath, body scanning—remain central to this approach. What changes is not the fundamental techniques but the framework around them: how they're taught, shared, and governed.

"Isn't Buddhist psychology already secular and effective?"

Buddhist psychology offers valuable insights into human experience and behavior. However, its presentation often blurs the line between secular and religious content, creating confusion and potential ethical issues in secular contexts. While concepts like conditioned arising or the nature of mind can be framed secularly, they're frequently taught alongside religious and metaphysical concepts. Open MBSR seeks clear boundaries, not to rejecting some of the ideas of Buddhist psychology, but to engage with it honestly and transparently. This clarity allows both secular and Buddhist approaches to thrive authentically rather than through subtle mixing.

"Isn't this disrespecting Jon Kabat-Zinn's work and legacy?"

On the contrary, Open MBSR represents the natural evolution of Jon Kabat-Zinn's revolutionary vision. Remember that MBSR itself was a radical departure from traditional Buddhist teaching methods. Kabat-Zinn dared to imagine a secular, scientific approach to mindfulness when many thought that impossible. Open MBSR continues this trajectory, addressing challenges that have emerged as MBSR grew beyond what any single person or institution could have envisioned.

"Who are you to challenge things and propose this? What is your lineage?"

This question itself reveals the hierarchy-based thinking we need to move beyond. The validity of these ideas doesn't rest on my authority, lineage, or qualifications; it rests on their merit and practical effectiveness. I'm not claiming special insight or demanding trust based on credentials. I'm offering a framework for discussion, evolution, and collective improvement. Judge these ideas on their substance. And if you have a valid concern? Bring it! Your lineage will not determine if your voice will be heard. Thoughtful critique from all sources is not only welcomed but cherished.

"Won't this devalue years of training and certification?"

Your training, experience, and hard-won insights remain invaluable. Open MBSR doesn't erase or devalue that knowledge; it creates new contexts for sharing it. Rather than depending on centralized certification, your credibility will rest on your demonstrable skills, practical wisdom, and ongoing contribution to the community. This actually gives experienced practitioners more opportunities to share their expertise, not fewer.

"Aren't you just creating a new power structure with yourself at the center?"

This concern goes to the heart of Open MBSR's principles. I have no interest in becoming a new guru or creating another hierarchy with myself at the top. My role is to articulate these ideas and help initiate change, and help the community. The very structure of Open MBSR, with its emphasis on transparency and distributed authority, is designed to prevent the concentration of power in any individual's hands, including mine.

"Isn't it irresponsible to change an evidence-based program?"

What's truly irresponsible is clinging to structures we know are problematic simply because they're familiar. Yes, MBSR is evidence-based, and that evidence shows the practices work. But evidence about practices doesn't validate organizational structures or teaching methods. Open MBSR maintains what research has validated while addressing issues of accessibility, power dynamics, and sustainability. As Open MBSR develops, we're committed to rigorous research examining its outcomes. This isn't reckless change; it's careful evolution guided by clear principles and collective wisdom.

These objections raise vital issues that will continue to inform how Open MBSR develops. They remind us to proceed thoughtfully, to honor what works while addressing what doesn't, and to remain open to ongoing dialogue and refinement. The path forward isn't about dismissing concerns; it's about addressing them honestly and creating something better together.

The Work at Every Level

Change happens through concrete choices, not abstract ideals. Here's what it might look like at every level.

Individual Practice

When you practice:

- Choose direct experience over guided recordings.
- Face silence without needing constant direction.
- Build skills rather than collecting experiences.
- Trust your own capacity for awareness.
- Question everything, especially comfort.

Teaching Differently

If you teach, your role isn't to become indispensable, it's to make yourself unnecessary. This means:

- Teaching actual meditation skills instead of leading guided journeys
- Reducing your guidance systematically
- Letting silence do its work
- Building student confidence through independence
- Creating clear paths to autonomy
- Not invoking an emotional state; remembering that mindfulness is about observing what is, good or bad, without judgment
- Avoiding religious language and political, one-dimensional, or metaphysical concepts

Creating New Communities

Communities concentrate power or distribute it; there's no middle ground. We're building spaces that:

- Foster independence while supporting each other
- Question authority as a practice, not a rebellion

- Share skills rather than create dependencies
- Evolve through collective wisdom, not guru guidance
- Outlast any individual teacher or leader

Look at your current mindfulness spaces. Are they building dependency or independence? Are they distributing power or concentrating it? Your next choice either reinforces old hierarchies or helps build something new.

Building New Systems

Yes, we'll have institutions. Yes, we'll have certifications. But they'll serve human flourishing rather than institutional power. This means:

- Transparent processes instead of hidden hierarchies
- Distributed authority instead of centralized control
- Community oversight instead of guru governance
- Clear ethical frameworks instead of unspoken rules
- Innovation balanced with integrity

The difference isn't whether we have structures, but how they operate. Every system either empowers or controls. We're building systems that liberate.

Maintaining Quality Without Hierarchy

"But won't quality suffer without centralized control?"

This question reveals how deeply we've internalized hierarchical thinking. We assume that quality requires authority, and that oversight demands power concentration. But what if the opposite is true? What if distributed responsibility creates stronger safeguards than centralized control?

Let's be clear: The risks of decentralization are real. Practices could become diluted. Teaching standards might vary wildly. Ethics could blur. But the solution isn't to recreate old hierarchies in new forms. It's to build systems that make quality everyone's responsibility.

Think of it like open-source software. Linux isn't reliable because some authority decreed it so. It's reliable because thousands of eyes watch for problems, because the community collectively maintains standards, because improvements can come from anywhere. Here's how this works in practice.

Clear standards, open evolution:

- Comprehensive documentation of core practices
- Transparent criteria for modifications
- Community review of adaptations
- Explicit ethical frameworks

Distributed quality control:

- Peer-review networks
- Regular practice audits
- Anonymous feedback channels
- Local community oversight

Collective teacher development:

- Skill progression pathways
- Ongoing peer supervision
- Documentation of experience
- Regular competency reviews

This isn't quality control through authority. It's quality assurance through transparency, community engagement, and shared responsibility. When everyone can see the standards, review the practices, and contribute to improvement, quality becomes cultural rather than enforced.

At the heart of this approach is transparency, making everything explicit. No hidden hierarchies. No unwritten rules. No guru-to-disciple transmission lines. When the framework is clear, when modifications are documented, when feedback paths are open, quality emerges from collective wisdom rather than individual authority.

This approach demands more from all of us. It's easier to follow rules than to engage in constant discernment. It's simpler to defer to authority than to take collective responsibility. But the reward is a practice that remains both potent and pure precisely because it's maintained by many hands rather than controlled by a few.

Quality without hierarchy isn't just possible, it's essential for mindfulness to truly serve human flourishing. The question isn't whether standards will be maintained, but whether we're ready to move from passive compliance to active stewardship of this transformative practice.

Protecting What We Build

History teaches us that movements often drift from their original vision. Already, we can see the threats:

- New gurus will emerge wearing the mask of independence.
- Old power structures will rebrand themselves as "open."
- McMindfulness will attempt to commoditize these approaches.

The greatest danger isn't opposition; it's subtle drift from principles to procedures, from genuine independence to comfortable conformity.

Beyond Good Intentions

Vision alone won't protect us. We need:

- Clear, transparent governance structures
- Explicit ethical frameworks that prevent power concentration
- Regular community review of our practices
- Systematic checks against guru-dynamics
- Built-in mechanisms for questioning authority

Each person involved helps protect this integrity by:

- Speaking up when principles are compromised
- Questioning practices that create dependency
- Contributing to protective frameworks
- Maintaining transparency in all processes
- Participating in community oversight

The Path Forward

This transformation happens through specific actions, not vague hopes. Here's what's next.

Immediate Steps

- Start practicing independently today.
- Begin reducing reliance on guided meditation.
- Connect with others interested in this approach.
- Question power dynamics in your current mindfulness spaces.
- Share these ideas where you can have impact.

Long-Term Development
- Help build peer-review Open MBSR certification processes.
- Contribute to quality assurance mechanisms.
- Participate in teacher training development.
- Engage in community governance.
- Support ethical framework creation.

From Blueprint to Reality

I began this book by exposing the hidden chains in modern mindfulness, the stealth Buddhism, the guru worship, the McMindfulness marketing machine. I traced how MBSR, born from revolutionary intentions, calcified into another hierarchy. But exposure without action changes nothing. The practices are tested. The framework exists. Now comes the real work of bringing it to life.

Key Takeaways

- Transforming mindfulness practice requires addressing legitimate concerns while maintaining forward momentum.
- Change happens at multiple levels simultaneously: individual practice, teaching approaches, community building, and institutional structures.
- Creating new systems requires both clear principles and robust protections against power concentration.
- The path forward involves both immediate actions and long-term development work.
- Success depends on collective engagement and continuous community oversight.

Reflection Questions

1. How could you begin implementing Open MBSR principles in your current practice or teaching?
2. What protective mechanisms would be most important in your local mindfulness community?
3. Where do you see opportunities to distribute rather than concentrate power in your mindfulness spaces?
4. What aspects of traditional MBSR could be preserved while implementing Open MBSR principles?
5. How might you contribute to the long-term development of Open MBSR?

Looking Ahead

The future of mindfulness stands at a crucial juncture. We can either watch as these practices become further commoditized and controlled, or we can actively participate in creating something different: a truly open, ethical, and transformative approach to human flourishing. The choice isn't between preserving tradition and embracing change, but between passive acceptance and active engagement in mindfulness's evolution. Through careful attention to legitimate concerns, clear implementation at every level, and robust protections against power concentration, we can create lasting change. The framework exists. The practices are tested. The community is forming. What happens next depends on all of us.

A Personal Note to Readers

As you reach the end of this book, I want to express my deep gratitude for your engagement with these ideas. Each of you brings unique experiences and perspectives to this work. That some concepts resonate while others challenge or disturb you isn't just natural—it's valuable. This diversity of responses will help shape Open MBSR's evolution.

Take time with these ideas. Question them. Disagree with parts while finding value in others. True understanding often unfolds gradually, and many concepts only become clear through direct experience. This isn't a doctrine to accept wholesale but a framework to explore, challenge, and refine.

While I hold deep conviction about this path—enough to write this book and advocate for change—I'm acutely aware that I'm just one voice in what must become a much larger conversation. My role is not to be an authority, but rather to spark dialogue, connect abstract ideals to practical approaches, and help weave together a community of practitioners and teachers.

Open MBSR must be shaped by many hands, hearts, and minds. It must draw from diverse experiences and evolve through collective wisdom. Your role—whether as practitioner, teacher, researcher, or curious explorer—is vital. Your questions, challenges, and even doubts will strengthen these ideas and help shape what Open MBSR ultimately becomes.

Engage with this work in whatever way feels authentic to you. Take what serves you, question what doesn't, and contribute your unique perspective. The future of mindfulness practice belongs to all of us. Together, we can create something transformative—not through following a single leader, but through our collective commitment to genuine, ethical, and liberating practice.

Thank you for being part of this journey. I look forward to learning from you as we make these possibilities real.

With gratitude and hope,

– Mo Edjlali

Notes

Chapter 3

1. The *Khuddakapāṭha* is a canonical text in the Pali Canon, comprising nine short discourses foundational to Buddhist practice. It is the first book of the *Khuddaka Nikāya* in the *Sutta Piṭaka*.
2. Siddhartha Gautama, commonly known as the Buddha, was a spiritual teacher and the founder of Buddhism. He lived in northern India between the 6th and 4th centuries BCE. His teachings form the foundation of Buddhist practice.
3. The *Satipaṭṭhāna Sutta* is a foundational discourse in the Pāli Canon, presenting the Buddha's teachings on the four establishments of mindfulness: contemplation of the body, feelings, mind, and mental phenomena.
4. The *Dhammacakkappavattana Sutta*, often translated as "Setting in Motion the Wheel of Dhamma," is traditionally regarded as the Buddha's first discourse following his enlightenment. In this seminal teaching, delivered at the Deer Park in Sarnath, the Buddha introduces the Middle Way, the Four Noble Truths, and the Noble Eightfold Path, laying the foundational framework for all subsequent Buddhist teachings.

Chapter 4

1. The GNU Project was launched in 1983 to create a free UNIX-like operating system, emphasizing users' rights to modify and share software. Its GNU General Public License (GPL) became a cornerstone of both the Free Software Movement and the open-source movement, which later adopted a more commercially oriented approach to collaborative development. While free software focuses on ethics and user freedom, open source highlights practical benefits for innovation (see gnu.org).

References

Adler, A. (1912). *The Neurotic Character*. Moffat, Yard and Co.

Barrett, L. F., and Simmons, W. K. (2015). "Interoceptive Predictions in the Brain." *Nature Reviews Neuroscience* 16(7): 419–429. https://doi.org/10.1038/nrn3950.

Beck, K., Beedle, M., van Bennekum, A., Cockburn, A., Cunningham, W., Fowler, M., Grenning, J., Highsmith, J., Hunt, A., Jeffries, R., Kern, J., Marick, B., Martin, R. C., Mellor, S., Schwaber, K., Sutherland, J., and Thomas, D. (2001). *Manifesto for Agile Software Development*. Agile Alliance. https://agilemanifesto.org/

Britton, W. B., Lindahl, J. R., Cooper, D. J., Canby, N. K., and Palitsky, R. (2021). "Defining and Measuring Meditation-Related Adverse Effects in Mindfulness-Based Programs." *Clinical Psychological Science* 9(6): 1185–1204.

Brown, C. G. (2019). *Debating Yoga and Mindfulness in Public Schools*. Chapel Hill: University of North Carolina Press.

Center for Mindfulness in Medicine, Health Care, and Society. (2014). *Mindfulness-Based Stress Reduction (MBSR): Standards of Practice*. University of Massachusetts Medical School.

Chen, C. (2022). *Work Pray Code: When Work Becomes Religion in Silicon Valley*. Princeton University Press.

Davidson, R. J., Kabat-Zinn, J., Schumacher, J., et al. (2003). "Alterations in Brain and Immune Function Produced by Mindfulness Meditation." *Psychosomatic Medicine* 65(4), 564–570.

Farias, M. and Wikholm, C. (2015). *The Buddha Pill: Can Meditation Change You?* London: Watkins.

Forbes, D. (2019). *Mindfulness and Its Discontents: Education, Self, and Social Transformation*. Fernwood Publishing.

Gazzaniga, M. S. (2011). *Who's in Charge?: Free Will and the Science of the Brain*. New York: Ecco.

Goldin, P. R., and Gross, J. J. (2010). "Effects of Mindfulness-Based Stress Reduction (MBSR) on Emotion Regulation in Social Anxiety Disorder." *Emotion* 10(1): 83–91

Hilton, L., et al. (2017). "Mindfulness Meditation for Chronic Pain: Systematic Review and Meta-Analysis." *Annals of Behavioral Medicine* 51(2): 199–213.

Hoffmann, M., Nagle, F., and Zhou, Y. "The Value of Open Source Software," Harvard Business School Working Paper, No. 24-038, January 1, 2024, https://www.hbs.edu/ris/Publication%20Files/24-038_51f8444f-502c-4139-8bf2-56eb4b65c58a.pdf.

Jha, A. P., Krompinger, J., and Baime, M. J. (2007). "Mindfulness Training Modifies Subsystems of Attention." *Cognitive, Affective, and Behavioral Neuroscience* 7(2): 109–119.

Kabat-Zinn, J. (1994). *Wherever You Go, There You Are: Mindfulness Meditation in Everyday Life*. New York: Hyperion.

Kabat-Zinn, J. (2011). "Some Reflections on the Origins of MBSR, Skillful Means, and the Trouble with Maps." *Contemporary Buddhism* 12(1): 281–306.

Kabat-Zinn, J. (2013). *Full Catastrophe Living: Using the Wisdom of Your Body and Mind to Face Stress, Pain, and Illness* (Revised and updated edition). New York: Bantam.

Kahneman, D. (2011). *Thinking, Fast and Slow*. New York: Farrar, Straus and Giroux.

Khoury, B., Sharma, M., Rush, S. E., and Fournier, C. (2015). "Mindfulness-Based Stress Reduction for Healthy Individuals: A Meta-Analysis." *Journal of Psychosomatic Research* 78(6): 519–528.

Korzybski, A. (1933). *Science and Sanity: An Introduction to Non-Aristotelian Systems and General Semantics*. New York: Institute of General Semantics.

Kucinskas, J. (2019). *The Mindful Elite: Mobilizing from the Inside Out*. New York: Oxford University Press.

Kurzban, R. (2012). *Why Everyone (Else) Is a Hypocrite: Evolution and the Modular Mind*. Princeton: Princeton University Press.

Langer, E. (2014). *Mindfulness* (25th Anniversary Edition). Boston: Da Capo Press.

LeDoux, J. (2015). *Anxious: Using the Brain to Understand and Treat Fear and Anxiety.* New York: Viking.

Lieberman, M. D. (2013). *Social: Why Our Brains Are Wired to Connect.* New York: Crown.

Marcuse, H. (1964). *One-Dimensional Man: Studies in the Ideology of Advanced Industrial Society.* Boston: Beacon Press.

Mill, J. S. (1859). *On Liberty.* London: John W. Parker and Son.

OpenLogic by Perforce and Open Source Initiative. "2022 State of Open Source Report." February 15, 2022. https://www.openlogic.com/system/files/ebook-openlogic-the-2022-state-of-open-source-report.pdf

Purser, R. (2019). *McMindfulness: How Mindfulness Became the New Capitalist Spirituality.* London: Repeater Books.

Santorelli, S. F., Meleo-Meyer, F., Koerbel, L., and Kabat-Zinn, J. (2017). *Mindfulness-Based Stress Reduction (MBSR) Authorized Curriculum Guide.* Center for Mindfulness in Medicine, Health Care, and Society, University of Massachusetts Medical School.

Sapolsky, R. M. (2017). *Behave: The Biology of Humans at Our Best and Worst.* New York: Penguin Press.

Schultz, W. (2015). "Neuronal Reward and Decision Signals: From Theories to Data." *Physiological Reviews* 95(3): 853–951.

Sellars, R. W., and Bragg, R. B. (May/June 1933). "A Humanist Manifesto," *The New Humanist* 6(3): 1–5, https://collections.carli.illinois.edu/digital/collection/mls_aha/id/1773/

Thompson, E. (2020). *Why I Am Not a Buddhist.* New Haven: Yale University Press.

Van Dam, N. T., van Vugt, M. K., Vago, D. R., et al. (2018). "Mind the Hype: A Critical Evaluation and Prescriptive Agenda for Research on Mindfulness and Meditation." *Perspectives on Psychological Science* 13(1): 36–61.

Acknowledgments

This book grew from the collective wisdom of many. I am deeply grateful to my brother, Cyrus, for his unwavering support, and to my dear friend Oxana, whose encouragement helped make this work possible.

The insights in these pages owe much to our team of MBSR teachers who gather regularly to discuss teaching methods, curriculum development, and the future of MBSR. Their dedication to preserving the integrity of MBSR while making it more accessible has been both inspiring and instructive. I am particularly thankful to our Certified Workplace Mindfulness advisory council members, whose expertise and guidance have been invaluable.

To the broader Mindful Leader community—the hundreds of thousands who have attended our events, participated in our training programs, read our articles, and engaged in thoughtful discussion—your engagement and feedback have shaped not just this book but the evolution of workplace mindfulness itself.

Thank you all for being part of this journey to make mindfulness more accessible, ethical, and transformative.

About the Author

Mo Edjlali is the founder and CEO of Mindful Leader, where he has pioneered innovative approaches to making mindfulness and meditation accessible in workplace settings. As the largest provider of MBSR (Mindfulness-Based Stress Reduction) training internationally, he oversees programming that has reached thousands of participants across dozens of countries.

He is the driving force behind the Mindful Leadership Summit, which annually convenes hundreds of leaders and change makers to explore the intersection of mindfulness, leadership, and organizational transformation. As both practitioner and innovator, Mo developed the Certified Workplace Mindfulness Facilitator program, now with over 550 alumni, creating new pathways for bringing mindfulness into modern workplaces. He created and launched Meditate Together to foster an international community of practice supporting daily meditation and habit formation.

Throughout his career, Mo has worked across industries, from government agencies and nonprofits to technology companies and Fortune 500 corporations, holding management and consulting positions at NASA, DHS, FICO, and Accenture. He has served on advisory boards for BrainFutures, Insight Meditation Community of Washington, DC, Insight on the Inside, Minds Incorporated, Think Impact, Art for Humanity, and Hungry for Music.

Mo brings a unique blend of technical expertise, business acumen, and contemplative practice to his work. As head editor at Mindful Leader, he has written extensively about challenges and opportunities in the mindfulness field, with particular focus on its integration into organizational settings. His computer engineering background from Virginia Tech, combined with years of mindfulness practice and teaching, allows him to bridge the practical and contemplative aspects of mindfulness training.

Through Open MBSR, Mo offers a fresh vision for making evidence-based mindfulness training more accessible, ethical, and adaptable to our rapidly changing world.

Index

Acceptance:
  in ACT Hexaflex, 68, 69
  in Buddhist philosophy, 47, 51, 52
  dialectical thinking about, 123, 127–129, 179
  in mindfulness, 4, 5
  in mindfulness meditation, 13
  misinterpreting, as conflict avoidance, 121
  in 9+1 Attitudes of Mindfulness, 164, 166
  in Nine Attitudes of Mindfulness, 25, 60
  passive, 52, 84, 211
  of positive attitudes, 111
Acceptance and Commitment Therapy (ACT), 67–70, 109
Accessibility:
  of algebra, 105
  balance of integrity and, 93–94
  of Buddhist philosophy, 45–49
  and commercialization, 146
  common language for, 14, 67, 84
  of corporate mindfulness, 133, 134, 148–149
  and cycle of exclusion, 143–144
  exclusion in mindfulness communities, 147–148
  improving, of mindfulness, xii, 1
  of MBSR, 27, 29–30, 89, 90
  McMindfulness and, 94–96
  of mindful hatha yoga, 58
  and mindfulness as luxury belief, 141–143
  in Open MBSR, 98, 160, 163, 191, 202
  of spiritual minimalism, 80
  and standardization paradox, 145
Accountability, 138, 153
ACT (Acceptance and Commitment Therapy), 67–70, 109
ACT Hexaflex, 68–69
Action through nonaction *(wei-wu-wei)*, 59, 60
Activism, 118
Adaptation:
  in Agile methodology, 70, 73
  for algebra, 105
  dialectical thinking about, 126

Adaptation *(Continued)*
  in MBSR, 45, 48, 51, 90
  oligarchy and stifled, 145, 147
  in Open MBSR, 24, 63, 160, 164, 173, 177, 180
Adler, Alfred, 136
Advanced training, for MBSR teachers, 38
Advocacy for change, 166
Agency, 82, 84
Agile Manifesto, 70–71
Agile methodology, 70–74, 168
Algebra, 105–106, 170
All-Day Practice Intensive (Open MBSR), 194
All-Day Silent Retreat (MBSR), 33
Allowing and Letting Be (week 5), 32
Altered states, pursuing, 9, 10
Amygdala, 114
Ānāpānasati (mindfulness of breathing), 43
Anatta (non-self), 55–56
Anicca (impermanence), 55
Appreciative joy *(muditā),* 53, 54, 60
Aristotle, 134
Artificial intelligence (AI), ix, 82, 105
Asanas, yogic, 56
Attitudinal foundations:
  MBSR, 25–26, 34, 41, 59–61, 127
  Open MBSR, 126, 160, 164–167
Authority, 139–140
Autonomy, 163, 182–183
Awareness of breath, 6, 42–43, 170, 184, 185

Barrett, Lisa Feldman, 113
Beginner's mind, 25, 59, 127, 165
Black-and-white thinking, *see* One-dimensional thinking
Bliss, 11
Body scan, 7, 43–44, 170, 184, 189–190
Boundaries:
  ethical, 182
  generosity and honoring, 166
  between secular and spiritual, 10, 97, 100, 180, 202
Breath, awareness of, 6, 42–43, 170, 184, 185
Breath regulation *(pranayama),* 56
Brewer, Judson, 18
Britton, Willoughby, 19
Brown, Candy Gunther, 92–93
Brown University, 29, 35, 37, 140
Buddha, *See* Gautama, Siddhartha
Buddha Jewel, 46
The Buddha Pill (Farias and Wikholm), 19, 65, 91
Buddhist entanglement problem, 87, 89–107
  abuse of spiritual power due to, 96–98
  algebra's universality as model for resolving, 105–106
  in Buddhist psychology, 98–100
  contemplative science to navigate, 66, 91–92
  derivation vs. recontextualization to resolve, 100–102
  McMindfulness critique of, 94–96

Siddhartha's rebellion as blueprint for resolving, 103–104
stealth Buddhism critique of, 92–94
transparency about Buddhist philosophy and MBSR, 102–103
Buddhist philosophy, 2, 41–62
awareness of breath in, 42–43
dialectical thinking in, 124
ehipassiko or invitation to investigate in, 51–52
Eightfold Path in, 48–49
Four Foundations of Mindfulness in, 49–51
Four Immeasurables in, 53–54
Four Noble Truths in, 48
loving-kindness in, 45
mindfulness as stealth Buddhism, 92–94
neural Buddhism, 65, 91
and Nine Attitudes of Mindfulness, 59–61
open awareness in, 44
origins of body scan in, 43–44
origins of core MBSR practices in, 41–45
problematic entanglement of secular mindfulness with (*see* Buddhist entanglement problem)
roots of mindfulness in, 12
separating secular mindfulness from, 98
synthesis of MBSR practices and, 61
Three Characteristics (Three Marks of Existence) in, 54–56
Three Jewels of, 45–48
transparency about MBSR and, 102–103
Buddhist psychology, 98–100, 202

Catholic Church, 97
Center for Inquiry, 82
Center for Mindfulness, 23, 28–30, 34–35
Certification, 38, 170–171, 203
Challenges, acknowledging, 166
Chan Buddhism, 59
Chen, Carolyn, 148–149
Choiceless awareness, 185
Circle of equals, 79
Citta (Mindfulness of Mind States), 50
Clarity, secular, 160, 161, 180
Clear instruction, 182, 186
Clear naming, 182
Closed thought systems, 111–112
Cognitive biases, 65, 109, 110, 115, 118, 119
Cognitive defusion, 69, 70
Collective wisdom:
Buddhist philosophy on, 47
in Open MBSR, 73, 79, 80, 164, 169, 208
in open-source revolution, 76
in Quakerism, 78–80
Commercialization, 1, 95, 146, 162, 174
Committed action, 69
Commodification, 95–97, 118, 146

Common language for, 15, 67, 84, 170
Communication Exercises, 187
Communities:
    creating Open MBSR, 205–206
    integrating dialectical thinking in, 128
    intentional, 161–162
    MBSR centered on, 150–153
    stewardship by, 180
    transformation of, 174
Compassion, 31, 38, 53, 54, 118
Complexity, xii
    in ACT, 69
    dialectical thinking to navigate, 123, 125, 126
    embracing, in Open MBSR, xii
    of human experience, 64, 109
    of mindfulness, 19
    one-dimensional thinking and denial of, 110–114
    Open MBSR Manifesto that embraces, 157, 160, 162, 173
    Open MBSR practices that embrace, 186
    shadow self and denial of, 120, 123
Confirmation bias, 65
Connection, power through, *see* Networks
Contemplative science, 64–67, 91–92
Contentment *(santoṣa)*, 59
Core practices:
    of MBSR, 41–45, 178–179, 183–184
    of Open MBSR, 178–179, 182–186, 202
Corporate mindfulness. *See also* workplace applications, of MBSR
    access and power in, 148–150
    as McMindfulness, 95–96, 168
    oligarchic control associated with, 133–134
    and politicization of mindfulness, 118
    as reconceptualization, 101
Critical engagement, 191
Critical thinking. *See also ehipassiko* (invitation to investigate)
    about MBSR, 19–20
    and compassion, 118
    dialectical thinking and, 124, 125
    embracing/integrating shadow part of mindfulness, 122, 123, 163
    nonjudging and, 165
    one-dimensional vs., 110–113, 115
    in secular humanism, 81–82
    skeptical inquiry and, 129
Cultural appropriation, 99, 106, 122
Culturally responsive MBSR, 106, 151–152
Customization, 151–152
Cutting through *(trekchö)*, 43

Daily life, integration in, 33, 161, 179, 186–188, 194
Dalai Lama, 65, 91

Daoism (Taoism), 59, 60, 124, 165
Darwin, Charles, 81
Davidson, Richard, 17, 18
Debate, 83, 105, 111–112, 117
Debating Yoga and Mindfulness in Public Schools (Brown), 92–93
Decentralization, 206–208
Default Mode Network (DMN), 114, 115
Democratization, 73, 76–77, 80, 144–145, 150, 151, 164
Dependency, xii, 154, 190, 195, 206
Dependent origination, xii, 56
Derivation, 100–102, 159–160, 168
Dewey, John, 81
Dhamma (Mindfulness of Phenomena), 50
Dhammacakkappavattana Sutta ("Setting in Motion the Wheel of Dhamma"), 55, 215n4
Dhamma Jewel, 46–47
Dhammapada, 60
Dhyana (meditation), 57
Dialectical thinking, 123–130, 163–167, 179
Difficult Communications Calendar, 187
Direct experience, learning from, *see* Experiential learning
Direct investigation, 51–52
Discernment, 78, 104, 160, 165–166, 208
Dispassion *(vairāgya),* 60
Distributed power structure, xii, 160, 179–180, 204, 207

Diverse perspectives:
  common language for, 14
  hidden networks and suppression of, 140–141
  in mindfulness communities, 147–148, 152–153, 163, 181, 195
  one-dimensional thinking and, 117, 118, 125, 128
  in Open MBSR, xiii, 67
  on research teams, 92
  of teachers, 38, 170–171
Divides, bridging, 118, 126
Divine abodes, 45
DMN (Default Mode Network), 114, 115
Dual processing, 113, 115
Dukkha (suffering), 48, 55

Echo chambers, 91, 117, 128, 147, 152–153
Economic gatekeeping, 133, 142–143, 151
Educational applications, of MBSR, 24, 29
Ehipassiko (invitation to investigate), 41, 51–52, 61, 102
Eightfold Path, 46, 48–49, 61, 215n4
Eight-week curriculum:
  MBSR, 30–34, 192
  Open MBSR, 191–195
Einstein, Albert, 81
Elitism, ix, 14, 134–136, 138, 142–143
Embodied Awareness (week 3), 193

Embodied mindfulness, 58
Emotional engagement, 166
Emotional evocation, 9, 10
Emotional regulation, 17
Empowerment, 139–140, 163, 182–183, 199
Engle, Adam, 65
Enlightenment, 81
Equality, 78
Equanimity *(upekkhā)*, 53, 54, 60
Ethical boundaries, 182
Ethical framework, 83, 100, 126, 136, 153
Ethical principles *(yamas* and *niyamas)*, 57
Evidence-based research, 16–19, 29, 163, 170–172, 202, 204
Evolutionary adaptation, one-dimensional thinking as, 114, 115
Exclusion, 140, 143–144, 147–148
Exclusivity, 15, 67, 95, 97, 122, 135, 139–144
Exercises, practices vs., 181–182
Expansive well-wishing, 185
Experiencing the Present Moment (week 3), 32
Experiential learning:
 dialectic of beginner's mind and, 127, 165
 in MBSR, 42, 51–52, 178
 in mindful hatha yoga, 58
 in Open MBSR, 164, 178
 in Quakerism, 78–79

Facilitator training, on dialectical thinking, 127–128
Faith *(saddhā)*, 60
Farias, Miguel, 19, 65, 91
Five core outcomes, 160–162
Five Hindrances, 50
Flexibility:
 ACT to cultivate psychological, 67–70
 dialectical thinking and cognitive, 123–127
 explicit frameworks for greater, 167–170
 in formats, 195
 in forms of inquiry, 191
 in mindfulness, 4–5
 neuroplasticity and cognitive, 116
 in Open MBSR, 72, 73, 76, 104, 160, 173, 197
 in secular humanism, 82
 shadow self and lack of moral, 120
Focused attention (FA), 7, 184, 185
Forbes, David, 19
Forking, in open source, 76
Foundational training, for MBSR teachers, 38
Four Foundations of Mindfulness, 41, 49–51, 61, 102
Four Immeasurables, 53–54, 61
Four Noble Truths, 41, 46, 48, 61, 102, 215n4
Fox, George, 77
Free Software Movement, 215n1
Freud, Sigmund, 81

Full Catastrophe Living
(Kabat-Zinn), 25, 27, 35, 41, 59

Gautama, Siddhartha (Buddha), 46, 103–104, 215n2
Gazzaniga, Michael, 114
Generosity, 25, 60, 166
GNU Project and Manifesto, 74, 215n1
Goal orientation, 166
Goldilocks zone, 73
Goldin, P.R., 17
Google, 29
Gradual progression, 9. *See also* Progressive independence
Gratitude, 25, 60, 166
Gross, J.J., 17
Group learning, 179
Growth, cultivating, 77, 125, 164
Guided imagery, 9, 10
Gurus:
  abuse of spiritual power by, 96–98
  Agile methodology and, 73
  authority and empowerment paradox for, 139–140, 150–151
  dethroning, 178
  and Open MBSR, 150–151, 162, 166, 173, 178, 189, 210
  Quaker view of, 78, 79

Hatha yoga, 57–58
Hayes, Steven C., 67
Healing and the Mind (TV series), 27

Healthcare applications, of MBSR, 24, 29
Heal Thy Self (Santorelli), 35
Henderson, Rob, 142
Heraclitus, 124
Hierarchy-based thinking. *See also* Oligarchic control
  distributed power in Open MBSR vs., 179–180
  maintaining quality without, 168, 206–208
  in MBSR, 159, 167
  objections to Open MBSR based in, 203, 204
  Quakerism as defiance of, 77–78
Hilton, L., 17
Holistic approach, 28, 49, 57–58, 123
Humanist Manifesto, 81
Humility, xiii, 124, 137

Ideological alignment, 111, 116–120, 125
Immediate implementation steps, 209
Impermanence *(anicca)*, 55
Inclusivity:
  hidden networks and, 140
  MBSR and challenges with, 36, 37
  in mindfulness communities, 15, 152–153
  one-dimensional thinking and, 125
  in Open MBSR framework, 24, 157, 159, 195

231

Index

Inclusivity (*Continued*)
  politicization and, 118
  through scientific framing, 66, 92
Independence, *see* Progressive independence
Individual practice, Open MBSR in, 205
Inferiority/superiority complex, 133, 136–141
Innate capacity, awakening, 4–6
Inner Explorer, 29
Innovation:
  balancing integrity and, 35, 38, 103
  by the Buddha, 104
  common language for, 15
  disparate source of inspiration for, 63, 64, 85–86
  explicit framework for, 167–170
  hidden networks and, 140
  institutional control and, 134, 138
  MBSR as, 28
  in Open MBSR, 72, 73, 102, 152, 179–180, 191
  in open-source movement, 75
  standardization paradox and, 146, 147
Inquiry, 83, 129, 188–191
Institutions, Open MBSR, 206
Integrated practices, from MBSR, 186–187
Integrating Mindfulness into Daily Life (week 7), 33
Integrity:
  balance of accessibility and, 93–94

in Buddhist psychology, 99, 160
consistency in MBSR for, 140
ethical governance for culture of, 153
maintaining spiritual and secular, 98, 157
for Open MBSR framework, 72, 168–169, 177
as principle of Open MBSR, 162–163, 173
protecting Open MBSR's, 160, 208–209
standards to maintain, 34, 35, 38
using an explicit framework to maintain, 168, 171
Intel, 29
Intellectual property, 134, 146, 152
Intentional community, 161–162
Introduction to Mindfulness (week 1), 31
Introduction to Open MBSR (week 1), 193
Investigate, invitation to, *see* Ehipassiko
Investigative exercises, from MBSR, 187
Iterative development, 71, 72

Jha, Amishi, 17, 18
Jung, Carl, 109, 120

Kabat-Zinn, Jon, 4, 15, 23, 25–29, 34–36, 38, 41, 57, 59, 89, 90, 93–94, 164, 165, 203
Kahneman, Daniel, 113
Kalama people, 51

Kamma, 54
Kapleau, Philip, 27
Kataññu Sutta, 60
Kataññutā (gratitude), 60
Kaya (Mindfulness of the Body), 50
Kāyagatāsati Sutta (Mindfulness of the Body Discourse), 43
Khantivadi Jataka, 59
Khoury, B., 16–17
Khuddakapāṭha, 46, 215n1
Korzybski, Alfred, 15
Kucinskas, Jaime, 135, 136
Kurtz, Paul, 82
Kurzban, Robert, 114

Langer, Ellen, 4–5
Lazar, Sara, 18
Leading questions, 190
LeDoux, Joseph, 114
Letting go, 25, 60, 164, 166
Lieberman, Matthew D., 114
Life force *(prana),* 56
Lineage, of Open MBSR, 203
Linux, 167–168, 207
Long-term implementation, 210
Loving-kindness, 45, 53, 54
Loving-kindness meditation *(metta),* 7, 45, 185
Loy, David, 94
Luxury beliefs, 97, 133, 141–145, 151
Luxury goods, 95, 142

Magga, 48
Mahayana Buddhism, 60

Mantra meditation, 7, 10–11
Marcuse, Herbert, 109, 110, 112
MBSR, *see* Mindfulness-Based Stress Reduction
MBSR Teacher Training, 24, 36–38, 170–171
McMindfulness:
  and acceptance with advocacy for change, 166
  critiques of, 19, 94–96
  dilution of MBSR by, 106, 167
  exposing, 210
  Open MBSR and, 170, 173
  protecting Open MBSR against, 208
McMindfulness (Purser), 94
Meditation. *See also* Mindfulness meditation
  common techniques in, 10–11
  defined, 6–8
  dhyana, 57
  loving-kindness, 7, 45, 185
  mantra, 7, 10–11
  mindfulness and, 6–8
  mountain/lake, 185–186
  non-mindfulness approaches to, 10–11
  silent, self-directed, 195–197
  vipassana, 56
  walking, 184
  yogic, 57
Metta (loving-kindness meditation), 7, 45, 185
Middle Way, 124, 215n4
Midway Feedback Exercise, 187
Mill, John Stuart, 117
Mind, as your teacher, 79

Mind and Life Institute, 65, 91
Mindful Communication and Relationships (week 6), 194
Mindful Eating, 187
"Mindful elite," 134–136
The Mindful Elite (Kucinskas), 135
Mindful hatha yoga, 57–59
Mindful Leader, xii, 29, 35, 37, 197
Mindful Leadership Summit, xii
Mindful movement (mindfulness practice), 7, 50, 170, 184
Mindfulness. *See also* Secular mindfulness
  attitudes of, 25–26, 34, 41, 59–61, 126, 129, 164–167
  awakening your innate capacity with, 4–6
  building blocks of, 76
  common language for, 15, 67, 84, 170
  confusion about terminology in, 14–16
  crossroads for, 159
  defined, 4–6
  Four Foundations of, 41, 49–51, 61, 102
  key characteristics of, 10
  meditation and, 6–8
  state vs. trait, 5
Mindfulness and Communication (week 6), 32
Mindfulness-Based Stress Reduction (MBSR), 23–40
  blueprint for, 25–26
  challenges and opportunities in future of, 35–36
  core practices in, 41–45, 178–179, 183–184
  derivation vs. recontextualization of, 100–102
  effectiveness of, xii
  ehipassiko and direct investigation in, 51–52
  eight-week curriculum for, 30–34, 192
  Four Foundations of Mindfulness in, 50–51
  Four Immeasurables in, 53–54
  Four Noble Truths and Eightfold Path in context of, 49
  goal of, 25
  history of, 26–28
  honoring roots of, 39 (*See also* Buddhist philosophy)
  impact of, 28–30
  influence of Three Jewels of Buddhism on, 46–48
  integrating dialectical thinking in, 127–130
  Nine Attitudes of Mindfulness in, 25–26, 34, 41, 59–61, 127, 129, 164–167
  oligarchy in, 139–141
  Open MBSR as building on foundation of, 1, 63–64
  practices and exercises from, in Open MBSR, 183–188
  principles of inquiry in, 188–189
  standards of practice for, 34–35, 145
  synthesis of Buddhist philosophy and practices in, 61

teacher training in, 24, 36–38, 170–171
Three Marks of Existence in, 55–56
trademarks on, 35
transparency about Buddhist philosophy and, 102–103
unique characteristics of, 26
yogic influences on, 56–59
Mindfulness-Based Stress Reduction (MBSR): Standards of Practice (Center for Mindfulness in Medicine, Health Care, and Society), 23, 34–35
The Mindfulness-Based Stress Reduction (MBSR) Authorized Curriculum Guide (Santorelli et al.), 23
The Mindfulness-Based Stress Reduction (MBSR) Authorized Curriculum Guide (Santorielli et al.), 30–34
Mindfulness bubble, 117
Mindfulness Center, 29, 35, 37, 140
Mindfulness in Daily Life (week 7), 194
Mindfulness meditation:
common anchors for, 10
defined, 8–10
effects of, 11, 13
mantras in, 10–11
myths about, 11–13
research on effects of, 16–19
Mindfulness movement (social movement), xi, xiii, 3, 87. *See also* Secular mindfulness
Mindfulness Network, 35
Mindfulness of Feelings *(vedana)*, 50
Mindfulness of Mind States *(citta)*, 50
Mindfulness of Phenomena *(dhamma)*, 50
Mindfulness of the Body *(kaya)*, 50
Mindfulness skills, practicing, 161
Mindful yoga, 42, 57–59
Minimum Viable Products (MVPs), 71
Mountain/lake meditation, 185–186
Muditā (appreciative joy), 53, 54, 60
Multidimensional thinking, 110, 116, 130
Musa al-Khwarizmi, Muhammad ibn, 105
MVPs (Minimum Viable Products), 71

Narrative creation, 114, 115
Neale, Miles, 94
Negative findings, reporting, 92
Nekkhamma (renunciation), 60
Networks, hidden/informal, 134, 140–141
Neural Buddhism, 65, 91
Neuro-elitism, 138
Nhất Hạnh, Thích, 27
Nibbana, 56

9+1 Attitudes of Mindfulness
(Open MBSR), 126,
164–167
Nine Attitudes of Mindfulness
(MBSR), 25–26, 34, 41,
59–61, 127, 129, 164–167
Nine Dots Exercise, 187
Nirodha, 48
Niyamas (ethical principles), 57
Noble Eightfold Path, *see*
Eightfold Path
Nonjudging:
and acceptance of positive
attitudes, 111
compassion and, 54
embodying, 38
in mindfulness, 4, 5
of mindfulness as luxury belief,
143
misusing, to bypass debate or
difficult emotions, 117,
121
in Nine attitudes of
Mindfulness, 25, 31, 59
in Open MBSR, 164, 165
Non-self *(anatta),* 55–56
Non-striving, 9, 25, 31, 60, 127,
166

OA, *see* Open awareness
Oasis Institute, 34, 37
Observing self, 69
Oligarchic control, 88, 133–156,
167, 169
community-centric vision
of MBSR to dismantle,
150–153

and guru paradox, 139–140
and inferiority/superiority
complex, 136–141
by mindful elite, 134–136
and mindfulness as luxury
belief, 141–145
and standardization paradox,
145–150
taking action to address,
153–154
via hidden networks, 140–141
"One-Dimensional Man"
(Marcuse), 110
One-dimensional thinking, 87,
109–132
brain's preference for, 113–116
dialectical thinking as remedy
to, 123–130
fundamental shift away from,
130
political ideology entrenched
in secular mindfulness,
116–120
and shadow aspects of self,
120–123
One-size-fits-all approaches, 145,
151–152, 154
On Liberty (Mill), 117
Open awareness (OA), 7, 44, 185
Open MBSR framework, xi, 1,
157–211
ACT influences on, 69–70
addressing oligarchic structures
in, 150–153
Agile influence on, 72–74
building, 173–174
common objections to, 201–204

concerns about stealth Buddhism in, 93
contemplative science influences on, 66–67
derivation in, 101–102
distinct elements of, 179–180
eight-week curriculum for, 191–195
evolution of, 181
exercises and practices in, 181–188
four pillars of, 173
implementation of (see Open MBSR implementation)
influences on, 2, 63–86
integration of, into daily life, 186–188
as living practice, 181
open source revolution's influence on, 74–77
progressive independence in, 195–197
Quaker influences on, 77–80
requirements to realize, 173–174
role of inquiry in, 188–191
secular humanist influences on, 80–85
teaching mindfulness in, 178–179
theoretical underpinnings of (see Open MBSR Manifesto)
Open MBSR implementation, 158, 170, 201–211
addressing common objections during, 201–204
at every level, 204–206
immediate steps for, 209
long-term, 210
maintaining quality without hierarchy during, 206–208
Mindful Leader resources for, 197
principles guiding, 198
protecting integrity of framework during, 208–209
Open MBSR Manifesto, 157, 159–176
on 9+1 attitudes of mindfulness in, 126, 164–167
building Open MBSR framework on, 173–174
on evidence-based research, 170–172
on five core outcomes, 160–162
flexibility of framework due to transparency of, 167–170
on seven guiding principles, 162–164
Open source revolution, 74–77, 152, 167–169, 207
Orientation sessions, 31, 192–193
Outcome-focused approach, Open MBSR as, 73

Paradoxes, 112, 126, 135
in ACT, 67–68
guru, 139–140, 150–151
in Open MBSR, 69
standardization, 145–150
Patience, 25, 59, 160, 165

Perception and Creative Responding (week 2), 32
Perception and Flexible Thinking (week 2), 193
Perens, Bruce, 75
Perfectionism, 13, 121
Performative enlightenment, 117
Performative perfection, 121
Personal commitment, 173
Personal growth, social responsibility and, 125
Personal interpretation, 66
Physical postures, of yoga, 56
Plato, 125
Pleasant and Unpleasant Events Calendar, 187
Politicization, 109, 111, 116–120, 123–125, 128
Positive attitudes, uncritical acceptance of, 111
Power concentration, 162, 204
Power structures. *See also* Oligarchic control
  Buddhist entanglement and abuse of, 96–98
  distributed, xii, 160, 179–180, 204, 207
  hidden, xi, xii
  and mindfulness meditation, 9–10
Practicality, of algebra, 105
Practices, exercises vs., 181–182
Prana (life force), 56
Pranayama (breath regulation), 56
Pre-class interview, MBSR, 31
Predictive processing, 113, 115

Prefrontal cortex, 114, 116, 125
Presence, 4, 5, 38, 69
Proactive change, 165
Problem solving, 125, 190
Progressive independence, 183, 186, 195–197
Projection, 120
Protestant Reformation, 97
Publication bias, 18, 91
Purposeful action, 65, 84, 127
Purser, Ronald, 19, 94
Quakerism, 77–80, 169
Quality control, 136, 207–208
Quick fix, mindfulness meditation as, 13

Radical transparency, 73, 76, 167–168
Raymond, Eric, 75
Reality, meditation to escape, 12
Reason, 81–84, 163. *See also* Secular humanism
Recontextualization, 100–102, 168
Reflective dialectic practice, 127
Reframing Nine Attitudes of Mindfulness, 127
Religious experience, mindfulness meditation as, 12
Renunciation *(nekkhamma)*, 60
Research, *see* Evidence-based research
Resilience:
  acknowledging challenges to build, 166
  loving-kindness to develop, 45
  MBSR to increase, 23, 28, 30, 33, 38

mindfulness to build, 3–5, 11, 13
Open MBSR to cultivate, 1, 64, 123, 129
reflective dialectic practices that foster, 127
understanding, 161, 193
Resistance to change, 121
Resistance to critique, 112, 117
Responsibility, 125, 153, 206–208
Reward reinforcement, 114–115
Right action, 49
Right concentration, 49
Right effort, 49
Right intention, 48
Right livelihood, 49
Right mindfulness, 49
Right speech, 49
Right view, 48

Saddhā (faith), 60
Sagan, Carl, 82
Samudaya, 48
Sangha Jewel, 48
Santorelli, Saki, 23, 35–38
Santoṣa (contentment), 59
Sapolsky, Robert, 114
Satipaṭṭhāna Sutta, 49, 215n3
Schultz, Wolfram, 114–115
Secular clarity, 160, 161, 180
Secular humanism, 80–85
Secular Humanist Manifesto III, 82
Secular mindfulness:
  Buddhist entanglement problem for, 89–107
  Buddhist psychology and, 202
  contemplative science and, 65
  in MBSR, 29, 60–61, 66, 89
  oligarchic control in, 133–156
  one-dimensional thinking as problem for, 109–132
  political ideology entrenched in, 116–120
  reclaiming, 118
  separating Buddhism and, 98
  three fundamental problems for, 87–88
Self:
  in ACT, 69
  shadow aspects of, 120–123
Self-directed practice, 195–197
Self-organization, 73
Self-reflection exercises, 187–188
Seung Sahn, 27
Seven Factors of Awakening, 50
Shadow aspects of self, 120–123
Shadow elements of MBSR, 159, 162, 164, 167, 169, 180. *See also* Buddhist entanglement problem; Oligarchic control; One-dimensional thinking
Shambhala International scandal, 137
Shikantaza (just sitting), 43
Shoshin, 59
Silence, 33, 78, 79, 139, 183, 195–197
Simplicity, 78, 80, 111, 113–116
Six-Month Letter, 188
Skeptical inquiry, 129
Social cognition, 114, 115
Social responsibility, 125

Social sorting, 144–145
Socratic method, 124
Spiritual bypassing, 117, 121, 164
Spirituality, superficial approach to, 19, 94–96
Spiritual materialism, xi, 133, 164, 173
Spiritual minimalism, 80
Spiritual teaching, by Open MBSR teachers, 190
Stability and adaptability reflection, 185–186
Stallman, Richard, 74
Standardization, 37, 134, 145–151, 154, 171, 207
State mindfulness, 5
Stealth Buddhism, 92–94, 167, 210
Stopping thoughts, 12
STOP Practice, 186
Stress: Responding vs. Reacting (week 4), 32
Stress, understanding, 161
Stress Reaction Cycle Exploration, 187
Stress reduction, 16–17. *See also* Mindfulness-Based Stress Reduction (MBSR)
Stress Reduction Clinic, 27
Stress response, one-dimensional thinking as, 114, 115
Suchness *(tathatā)*, 60
Suffering *(dukkha)*, 48, 55
Superficial approach to spirituality, 19, 94–96

Sustaining Practice and Moving Forward (week 8), 194–195
Sustaining the Practice (week 8), 33
System 1 and 2 thinking, 113

Taoism, *see* Daoism
Tathatā (suchness), 60
Teacher:
  embodiment of principles by, 179
  in Open MBSR framework, 173, 177–179, 205
  role of, 190–191
Teacher training:
  on dialectical thinking, 127–128
  MBSR, 24, 36–38, 170–171
  Open MBSR, 203, 207
Therapeutic interpretation, 190
Theravada Buddhism, 43, 49–50
Thinking, Fast and Slow (Kahneman), 113
Thompson, Evan, 65, 91
Three Characteristics (Three Marks of Existence), 54–56, 61
Three Jewels of Buddhist philosophy, 45–48, 61, 102
Tibetan Buddhism, 43
Toxic positivity, 121, 166, 173
Trait mindfulness, 5
Transcendental Meditation, 10, 11
Transformation:
  in AI revolution, xii

Buddhist entanglement and MBSR's potential for, 96, 98, 102–104
in Buddhist philosophy, 45, 47, 48, 56
community, 174
with MBSR, xii, 24, 25, 30, 33, 34, 41
in MBSR teacher training, 38, 39
with mindfulness, 1, 3, 5, 9, 16
oligarchic control and potential for, 134, 142–146, 148, 149, 154
one-dimensional thinking and potential for, 111–113, 119, 123–126
in Open MBSR framework, 64, 72, 157–160, 173, 182–183, 202
in open-source revolution, 74, 75

Transparency:
about Buddhist roots of MBSR, 42, 45, 91, 92, 102–103
about commercialization, 97
about inspiration for Open MBSR, 64
ethical governance and, 153
in evaluation of Open MBSR, 171–172
in Open MBSR, 36, 73, 74, 76, 162–163, 167–170, 182–183, 199, 204, 208
in open-source movement, 75
radical, 73, 76, 167–168

Trekchö (cutting through), 43
Trungpa, Chögyam, 137
Trust, 25, 60, 165–166

Uncertainty, 172, 181
Understanding Stress and Resilience (week 4), 193–194
Unity of opposites, 124
Universality, 105–106, 118, 119
University of California, San Diego, 35, 37
University of Massachusetts Medical Center, 2, 23, 25, 28–30, 34–36, 89, 170
Upekkhā (equanimity), 53, 54, 60
"Us versus them" mentality, 119

Vairāgya (dispassion), 60
Validation seeking, 190
Values, 69
Van Dam, Nicholas, 19
Varela, Francisco, 65
Vedanā (Mindfulness of Feelings), 50
Vipassana meditation, 56
Visualization, 7, 185–186

Walking meditation, 184
Walsh, Zack, 94
Wandering mind, guiding, 8–9
Waterfall methodology, 70
Wei-wu-wei (action through nonaction), 59, 60

Wherever You Go, There You Are (Kabat-Zinn), 27
Why I Am Not a Buddhist (Thompson), 91
Wikholm, Catherine, 19, 65, 91
Working with Thoughts and Emotions (week 5), 194
Workplace applications, of MBSR, 24, 28, 29, 95, 133–134, 148–150. *See also* Corporate mindfulness

Work Pray Code (Chen), 148–149

Yamas (ethical principles), 57
Yathābhūta-ñāṇadassana (seeing things as they are), 60
Yin and yang, 124, 165
Yoga, 41, 42, 56–59

Zen Buddhism, 43, 59